Library
Carroll
1601 Washington Road
Westminster, Maryland 21157

W9-BCI-573

WITHDRAWN

Books by W. S. Merwin

POEMS

Selected Poems *1988*
The Rain in the Trees *1988*
Opening the Hand *1983*
Finding the Islands *1982*
The Compass Flower *1977*
The First Four Books of Poems *1975*
(INCLUDING THE COMPLETE TEXTS OF
*A Mask for Janus, The Dancing Bears,
Green with Beasts* AND *The Drunk in the Furnace*)
Writings to an Unfinished Accompaniment *1973*
The Carrier of Ladders *1970*
The Lice *1967*
The Moving Target *1963*
The Drunk in the Furnace *1960*
Green With Beasts *1956*
The Dancing Bears *1954*
A Mask for Janus *1952*

PROSE

Unframed Originals *1982*
Houses and Travellers *1977*
The Miner's Pale Children *1970*

TRANSLATIONS

From the Spanish Morning *1985*
Four French Plays *1985*
Selected Translations 1968–1978 *1979*
Osip Mandelstam, Selected Poems
   (WITH CLARENCE BROWN) *1974*
Asian Figures *1973*
Transparence of the World (Poems by Jean Follain) *1969*
Voices (Poems by Antonio Porchia) *1969 1988*
*Products of the Perfected Civilization
(Selected Writings of Chamfort)* *1969*
*Twenty Love Poems and a Song of Despair
(Poems by Pablo Neruda)* *1969*
Selected Translations 1948–1968 *1968*
The Song of Roland *1963*
The Satires of Persius *1960*
The Poem of the Cid *1959*

W.S. MERWIN
SELECTED
POEMS

W. S. MERWIN
SELECTED
POEMS

ATHENEUM

New York

Poems from the following previously published books are included in this volume of *Selected Poems*:

A MASK FOR JANUS: copyright 1952 by Yale University Press
THE DANCING BEARS: copyright 1954 by Yale University Press
GREEN WITH BEASTS: copyright © 1955, 1956 by W.S. Merwin
THE DRUNK IN THE FURNACE: copyright © 1956, 1957, 1958, 1959, 1960
    by W.S. Merwin
THE MOVING TARGET: copyright © 1960, 1961, 1962, 1963 by W.S. Merwin
THE LICE: copyright © 1963, 1964, 1965, 1966, 1967 by W.S. Merwin
THE CARRIER OF LADDERS: copyright © 1967, 1968, 1969, 1970 by W.S. Merwin
WRITINGS TO AN UNFINISHED ACCOMPANIMENT: copyright © 1969, 1970,
    1971, 1972, 1973 by W.S. Merwin
THE COMPASS FLOWER: copyright © 1977 by W.S. Merwin
OPENING THE HAND: copyright © 1983 by W.S. Merwin
        SELECTED POEMS copyright © 1988 by W.S. Merwin

All rights reserved. No part of this book may be reproduced or transmitted in any form or by any means, electronic or mechanical, including photocopying, recording or by any information storage and retrieval system, without permission in writing from the publisher.

ATHENEUM
Macmillan Publishing Company
866 Third Avenue, New York, N.Y. 10022
Collier Macmillan Canada, Inc.

Library of Congress Cataloging-in-Publication Data

Merwin, W. S. (William Stanley), ———
    [Poems. Selections]
    Selected poems / W.S. Merwin.
        p. cm.
    Reprints from collections originally published 1952-1983.
    ISBN 0-689-11970-4.   ISBN 0-689-70736-3 (pbk.)
    I. Title.
    PS3563.E75A6   1988
    811'.54—dc19   87-31771
                                                                         CIP

Macmillan books are available at special discounts for bulk purchases for sales promotions, premiums, fund-raising, or educational use. For details, contact:

Special Sales Director
Macmillan Publishing Company
866 Third Avenue
New York, N.Y. 10022

Designed by Harry Ford

10   9   8   7   6   5   4

Printed in the United States of America

For Paula

NOTE

A selection of poems, and particularly poems written by some earlier version of oneself, is bound to be made up of latter-day choices that are primarily subjective.

For years I resisted making such a selection, partly because each of the successive volumes of poems that I published seemed to me distinct, and I did not want a general selection to blur the character of the separate books. But in time selections are inevitable, and the volumes from which these choices are made are there for those who may want them.

I have not changed the poems I have included. That is not because I thought they were beyond improvement but because in certain respects I am no longer the person who wrote them.

W S M

CONTENTS

From THE MOVING TARGET *(1963)*

From THE LICE *(1967)*

From THE CARRIER OF LADDERS *(1970)*

From WRITINGS TO AN UNFINISHED ACCOMPANIMENT *(1973)*

From THE COMPASS FLOWER *(1977)*

Contents

From A Mask for Janus *1952*

BALLAD OF JOHN CABLE AND THREE GENTLEMEN

He that had come that morning,
One after the other,
Over seven hills,
Each of a new color,

Came now by the last tree,
By the red-colored valley,
To a gray river
Wide as the sea.

There at the shingle
A listing wherry
Awash with dark water;
What should it carry?

There on the shelving,
Three dark gentlemen.
Might they direct him?
Three gentlemen.

"Cable, friend John, John Cable,"
When they saw him they said,
"Come and be company
As far as the far side."

"Come follow the feet," they said,
"Of your family,
Of your old father
That came already this way."

But Cable said, "First I must go
Once to my sister again;
What will she do come spring
And no man on her garden?

She will say 'Weeds are alive
From here to the Stream of Friday;
I grieve for my brother's plowing,'
Then break and cry."

"Lose no sleep," they said, "for that fallow:
She will say before summer,
'I can get me a daylong man,
Do better than a brother.' "

Cable said, "I think of my wife:
Dearly she needs consoling;
I must go back for a little
For fear she die of grieving."

"Cable," they said, "John Cable,
Ask no such wild favor;
Still, if you fear she die soon,
The boat might wait for her."

But Cable said, "I remember:
Out of charity let me
Go shore up my poorly mother,
Cries all afternoon."

They said, "She is old and far,
Far and rheumy with years,
And, if you like, we shall take
No note of her tears."

But Cable said, "I am neither
Your hired man nor maid,
Your dog nor shadow
Nor your ape to be led."

He said, "I must go back:
Once I heard someone say
That the hollow Stream of Friday
Is a rank place to lie;

And this word, now I remember,
Makes me sorry: have you
Thought of my own body
I was always good to?

The frame that was my devotion
And my blessing was,
The straight bole whose limbs
Were long as stories—

Now, poor thing, left in the dirt
By the Stream of Friday
Might not remember me
Half tenderly."

They let him nurse no worry;
They said, "We give you our word:
Poor thing is made of patience;
Will not say a word."

"Cable, friend John, John Cable,"
After this they said,
"Come with no company
To the far side.

To a populous place,
A dense city
That shall not be changed
Before much sorrow dry."

Over shaking water
Toward the feet of his father,
Leaving the hills' color
And his poorly mother

And his wife at grieving
And his sister's fallow
And his body lying
In the rank hollow,

Now Cable is carried
On the dark river;
Nor even a shadow
Followed him over.

On the wide river
Gray as the sea
Flags of white water
Are his company.

MENG TZU'S SONG

The sparrows gleaning gutters
Kick and shuffle the horsehair,
And the simple wind that stirs
Their feathers stirs my hair.

How can I know, now forty
Years have shuffled my shoulders,
Whether my mind is steady
Or quakes as the wind stirs?

Because one sparrow, running
On the old wind-ruts, can be
Turned by an unseen thing,
A small wind in the sky,

And changes, it sets me thinking;
Yet I know not if my mind
Is moved, or is but sinking
Alone to its own kind.

If my mind moves not in wind
Or other breaths, it is not
Strange; at forty the mind
Of Kao Tzu wavered not.

Lo, how is the kept wind let
Out to make trouble with me!
How can one remain not
Moving before his eye?

One cultivates bravery
That the skin's hair not flinch
Nor the frail eye flee
Nor the blood blanch.

One is as the trodden inch
Of horsehair on the bare ground
At the market place: wrench
Nor kick wring from him sound.

Thinks he as though he were sand
Or horsehair, should the stiff sword
Shave the strength from his mind
And stab away his word.

Thinks of defeat and blood,
All hairs blown from control,
The hands like hair in mud
As though it mattered little.

How can the thin mind be able?
How put off quaking only,
Keeping all else simple,
Even in wind steady?

The wind is stiff and is high.
Simple the wind. The open
Coat of horsehair on three
Sides flaps without passion.

DICTUM: FOR A MASQUE OF DELUGE

There will be the cough before the silence, then
Expectation; and the hush of portent
Must be welcomed by a diffident music
Lisping and dividing its renewals;
Shadows will lengthen and sway, and, casually
As in a latitude of diversion
Where growth is topiary, and the relaxed horizons
Are accustomed to the trespass of surprise,
One with a mask of Ignorance will appear
Musing on the wind's strange pregnancy.

And to him one must enter from the south
In a feigned haste, with disaster on his lips,
And tales of distended seas, continents
Submerged, worlds drowned, and of drownings
In mirrors; unto this foreboding
Let them add sidelong but increasing mention,
With darkening syllables, of shadows, as though
They stood and traded restlessness beneath
A gathering dark, until their figures seem
But a flutter of speech down an expense of wind.

So, with talk, like a blather of rain, begun,
Weather will break and the artful world will rush
Incontinent. There must be a vessel.
There must be rummage and shuffling for salvation
Till on that stage and violence, among
Curtains of tempest and shaking sea,
A covered basket, where a child might lie,
Timbered with osiers and floated on a shadow,
Glides adrift, as improbably sailing
As a lotus flower bearing a bull.

Hills are to be forgotten; the patter of speech
Must lilt upon flatness. The beasts will come;
And as they come, let one man, by the ark,
Drunken with desolation, his tongue
Rounding the full statement of the seasons,
Tremble and stare, his eyes seeming to chase
A final clatter of doomed crows, to seek
An affirmation, a mercy, an island,

Or hills crested with towns, and to find only
Cities of cloud already crumbling.

And these the beasts: the bull from the lotus flower
With wings at his shoulders; and a goat, winged;
A serpent undulating in the air;
A lion with wings like falling leaves;
These are to wheel on a winged wheel above
The sullen ark, while hare, swine, crocodile,
Camel and mouse come; and the sole man, always,
Lurches on childish limbs above the basket—
To his mere humanity seas shall not attain
With tempest, nor the obscure sky with torches.

(Why is it rumored that these beasts come in pairs
When the anatomies of their existence
Are wrought for singularity? They walk
Beside their shadows; their best motions are
Figments on the drapery of the air.
Their propagation is a redoubling
Merely of dark against the wall, a planetary
Leaning in the night unto their shadows
And stiffening to the moment of eclipse;
Shadows will be their lean progeny.)

At last the sigh of recession: the land
Wells from the water; the beasts depart; the man
Whose shocked speech must conjure a landscape
As of some country where the dead years keep
A circle of silence, a drying vista of ruin,
Musters himself, rises, and stumbling after
The dwindling beasts, under the all-colored
Paper rainbow, whose arc he sees as promise,
Moves in an amazement of resurrection,
Solitary, impoverished, renewed.

A falling frond may seem all trees. If so
We know the tone of falling. We shall find
Dictions for rising, words for departure;
And time will be sufficient before that revel
To teach an order and rehearse the days
Till the days are accomplished: so now the dove

Makes assignations with the olive tree,
Slurs with her voice the gestures of the time:
The day foundering, the dropping sun
Heavy, the wind a low portent of rain.

From The Dancing Bears *1954*

EAST OF THE SUN AND
WEST OF THE MOON

Say the year is the year of the phoenix.
Ordinary sun and common moon,
Turn as they may, are too mysterious
Unless such as are neither sun nor moon
Assume their masks and orbits and evolve
Neither a solar nor a lunar story
But a tale that might be human. What is a man
That a man may recognize, unless the inhuman
Sun and moon, wearing the masks of a man,
Weave before him such a tale as he
—Finding his own face in the strange story—
Mistakes by metaphor and calls his own,
Smiling, as on a familiar mystery?

The moon was thin as a poor man's daughter
At the end of autumn. A white bear came walking
On a Thursday evening at the end of autumn,
Knocked at a poor man's door in a deep wood,
And, "Charity," when the man came he said,
"And the thin hand of a girl have brought me here.
Winter will come, and the vixen wind," he said,
"And what have you but too many mouths to feed,
Oh what have you but a coat like zither-strings
To ward that fury from your family?
But I though wintry shall be bountiful
Of furs and banquets, coins like summer days,
Grant me but the hand of your youngest daughter."

"By a swooning candle, in my porchless door,
While all I wedded or sired huddle behind me,
The night unceremonious with my hair,
I know I cut a poor figure," the man said;
"And I admit that your cajolery
(For opulence was once my setting-on)
Finds me not deaf; but I must ask my daughter.
And no, she says. But come again on Thursday:
She is more beautiful than the story goes,
And a girl who wants a week for her persuading
Merits that slow extravagance," he said.
Further in autumn by a week's persuading
The youngest girl on a white bear went riding.

The moon played in a painted elder tree;
He said, when they had gone a while, "We walk
In a night so white and black, how can you tell
My shoulder from a moon-struck hill, my shadow
From the towering darkness; are you not afraid?"
And, "You are thin and colorful who ride
Alone on a white and monstrous thing; suppose
I rose up savage in a desolate place;
Are you not afraid?" And, "What if I were to wander
Down a black ladder, in a trope of death,
Through seven doors all of black ice, and come
On a land of hyperbole, stiff with extremes;
Would it not make the hair rise on your head?"

The wind with moonlit teeth rippled and sulked
In the paper trees, but three times "No," she said.
"Oh then hold fast by the hair of my shoulders,"
He said; "hold fast my hair, my savage hair;
And let your shadow as we go hold fast
The hair of my shadow, and all will be well."
Later than owls, all night, a winter night,
They traveled then, until the screaming wind
Fell behind or dead, till no stars glittered
In the headlong dark; and each step dark and long
As falling in the valley of the blind;
Yet all the while she felt her yellow hair
Hang loose at her shoulders, as though she stood still.

They came before daylight to a stone hill
Steep as a pier glass, where no shrub grew,
Nor grass rustled, nor breeze stirred before dawn.
When the bear knocked, a door swung wide. Their eyes
Enormous with the dark, a hall they entered
That blazed between mirrors, between pilasters
Of yellow chrysolite; on walls of brass
Gold branches of dead genealogies
Clutched candles and wild torches whence the flames
Rose still as brilliants. Under a fiery
Garnet tree with leaves of glass, sunken
In a pool of sea-green beryl as in still water
A gold salmon hung. And no sound came.

The wall healed behind them. When she turned,
The wall steep as a pier glass, the door
Vanished like a face in ruffled water,
And they stood dumb in the echoing light
While no flame crackled, no water fell. They passed
Between the rows of burning, between the rings
Of extinct animals that stared from sockets
In the braziered walls; hour upon hour,
Hall upon blazing hall, and came at last
Through obsequious curtains to a closed room
Where she descended; at a beck of his head
A gold table leapt from the air; she dined
That night on lapwing and wine of pomegranates.

The bear had gone. She touched a silver bell.
She stood straightway in a white chamber
By a bed of lapis lazuli. Red agate
And yellow chrysolite the floors. A white
Carnelian window gave upon cut hills
Of amethyst and yellow serpentine
Pretending summer; when she stood naked there
Her nakedness from the lighted stones
Sprang a thousand times as girl or woman,
Child or staring hag. The lamps went black;
When she lay down to sleep, a young man came
Who stayed all night in the dark beside her
But was gone before dawn came to that country.

Nightly he came again. Once he said,
"I am the white bear, who once was a man;
In a christian body, in a green kingdom
One time I had dominion. Now I keep
Not so much as the shadow that I had,
And my own shape only by dark; by day
Compelled I am to that pale beast. Let it be
Ensample to your forbearance: here love
Must wander blind or with mistaken eyes,
For dissolution walks among the light
And vision is the sire of vanishing."
What love soever in the dark there were,
Always at daylight she wakened alone.

By day she walked in the espaliered garden
Among pheasants and clear flowers; she said,
"What if these pheasants amble in white glass,
Ducks strut ridiculous in stone, the streams
Slither nowhere in beryl; why should I
Complain of such inflexible content,
Presume to shudder at such serenity,
Who walk in some ancestral fantasy,
Lunar extravagance, or lost pagoda
That dreams of no discipline but indolence?
What shall be rigid but gems and details
While all dimensions dance in the same air?
And what am I if the story be not real?

But what it is," she said, "to wander in silence,
Though silence be a garden. What shall I say,
How chiseled the tongue soever, and how schooled
In sharp diphthongs and suasive rhetorics,
To the echoless air of this sufficiency?
Where should I find the sovereign aspirate
To rouse in this world a tinkle of syllables,
Or what shall I sing to crystal ears, and where
All songs drop in the air like stones; oh what
Shall I do while the white tongued flowers shout
Impossible silence on the impossible air
But wander with my hands over my ears?
And what am I if the story be not real?

He says the place is innocent; and yet
I may not see his face; claims he is held
Equivocating between prince and beast
By the ministrations of an evil stepdame,
But such might be mere glittering deviltry.
Here is no nightly moon or tidal water
But mornings miming at mutability
Where all stands new at noon and nothing fades
Down the perfect amber of the afternoons;
All, simultaneous and unwearied, comes
Guesting again at evening. But a day
Must dwindle before dawn be real again;
And what am I if the story be not real?"

She said at night when he lay beside her,
"Why should I raise the singular dissent
Who delight in an undiminished country
Where all that was or shall be transitory
Stands whole again already? Yet I sigh
For snipes to whir and fall, for hawks to fall,
For one more mortal crimson that will fade,
For one glimpse of the twisted holly tree
Before my mother's door, and the short-lived
Wren by my mother's window, and the tame crane
Walking in shallow water. I would learn
Whether I dreamed then or walk now in a dream,
For what am I if the story be not real?"

Suddenly where no sound had been she heard
A distant lisp and crumble, like a wave,
Like the whisper of tidal water, emulous
Of its own whispers: his echoing heart. "Shall I
Pace an eternity of corridors,
Alone among sad topaz, the reflections
Flickering only on your emptiness,
And the soundlessness be like a sound of mourning,
That seemed a sound of joy? Nevertheless,
Go you shall if you wish; but promise,
Lest a malicious word undo us both,
Never to walk or talk alone," he said,
"With your mother, who is as wise as you."

It was a Sunday. Gold on the glass leaves.
She sat in the garden on the white bear's shoulders.
She touched a silver bell, and instantly
Saw the swaying of incorrigible meadows
Ripening, a green wind playful in barley,
The holly, contorted at her mother's door,
The fluttering wren—the brief feathers
Provisional about mortality—
At her mother's window, the tame crane walking
As though not real where the real shallows ran.
She had descended; the bear was gone;
She heard the whistling grass, and the holly leaves
Saying, "Your mother, who is wise as you."

She was greeted like a lost season.
Daylong she walked again in affluent summer,
But one day walked at last aside, and talked
Alone with her mother, who was wise as she.
"Equivocation between prince and beast,
The ministrations of an evil stepdame,
Might be a devilish tale; how could you tell,"
Her mother said, "should it be the devil's self
Or some marvel of ugliness you lay beside?
Take, better than advice, this end of candle
To light when he sleeps next you in the dark;
Only be careful that no drops fall."
The grass might whistle under the holly leaves.

On a day of no clouds he came to fetch her.
It was a Sunday. A soft wind stroking
The fields already white almost to harvest.
"Shall we not ride a while in the mortal air
Before we go," he asked, "for the love of fading?
But wish, when you are weary, for the sound
Of the silver bell, and we shall instantly
Be home again. Did all happen as I said?"
"Yes," she said, "how might it be otherwise?"
"Did you, then, walk aside with your mother?" he asked;
"Did you listen to your mother's advice?"
"Oh no," she said. "Then all may yet be well."
But she wished for the sound of the silver bell.

That night when she was sure he slept
She rose in the dark and struck light
To the end of candle, and held it above his face.
What blaze was this, what prince shaming with beauty
The sun peerless at noon? The dazzled stones
Seemed each a blond particular summer wringing
In the one thirst the lion and the nightingale.
The shadows bowed; they fell down amazed.
"And I with my foolish arm upraised . . .
But love so beggars me of continence,
Either I must kiss him or die," she said,
And bent, therewith, and kissed his head. Three times
The tallow folly from the candle fell.

"Oh why must all hope resolve to vanity?"
Waking, he cried; "Why could you not entertain
A curious patience but for one whole year,
For then had we been saved, and my spell broken.
Now this kingdom must shatter and I depart
For the wheeling castle of my stepmother
And marry a princess with a nose three ells long,
When I might have married you." "Oh love," she cried,
"May I not learn the way and follow you?"
"There is no way there that a body might follow;
Farther than dreams that palace lies,
East of the sun and west of the moon, girt
With rage of stars for sea. There no one comes."

She seemed to sleep, for she woke again
On a usual morning in a different world,
Bright grass blowing, birds loud in the trees;
That precious kingdom, that charmed lover
Gone. She was kneeling under a willow
In her salt tears. When she had called
And cried till she was weary she walked on
Slowly, walked the length of a day, and seemed
None the more weary for all her walking
But traveled, it seemed, in a landscape of exceptions
Where no evening came but a shadowy
Skeptical bird who settled in a tree
And sang, "All magic is but metaphor."

Under a crag, when it should have been evening,
Where there should have been shadows, by an apple tree,
She saw a hag who laughed to herself and tossed
A golden apple. "Good day, hag," she said.
"Can you tell me how I might find the castle
That lies east of the sun and west of the moon?"
"Whoever comes and calls me hag, haggard
May she sit also, unless it be the lady
Who should marry the prince there. Are you she?
Yes, she says. Yet the way I cannot tell.
Take, rather, this gold apple, mount this horse
To ride to ask my sister, and once there,
Tap him behind the left ear; he will come home."

Long she rode as the patience of stones
And saw again, when it should have been evening,
A hag who played with a golden carding comb.
"If withering were a signature of wisdom,
I were a miracle of sagacity,"
She said, "my brow invisible with laurel,
But I am bare parchment where a word might be,
And any road that might lead to that castle
Is a thing I never knew. All I can offer
By way of blessing is this gold carding comb,
But you might ask my sister; take my own horse.
When he has brought you where she sits, tap him
Behind the left ear; he will come home again."

The third hag said, "I have been young as you,
And shall be so again, unless the stars
Tell lies in the shifty dark, but whether
More pleasure is to be young and pass for fair
Or to be haggard and seem knowledgeable,
I am too wise to choose, and yet the way
That castle lies is a thing I never knew;
But there you will come, late or never. I give you,
Beside that wisdom, this golden spinning wheel,
And if you wish, you may ride my own horse
To ask the East Wind. When you are there,
Tap the beast once behind the left ear,
And he will be off and come to me again."

Oh then she rode such waste of calendars
She should have found the end of weariness
But came instead to the house of the East Wind.
"Oh Wind," she called, "which way would you blow,
Which way might I follow to come to the castle
That lies east of the sun and west of the moon?"
"I, bold of wing beyond the glimpse of morning,
Have found the dark where no birds sleep,
Have shivered and returned, have many times
Heard of that castle, but never blown so far
Nor learned the way. But I have a brother," he said,
"An infinite voyager: be pleased to sit
Between my shoulders and I shall take you there."

Though faster then than summoned ghosts they flew,
Long was that journey as the wisdom of owls
Before they came to the roof of the West Wind.
"For all I am prodigious of voyages,
Whistle heyday and holiday, make light
Of the poor limbs of summer and have sailed
Beyond the hueless sighing of drowned days
Into the dark where no shades sigh,
Have shuddered and come home a different way,
Unholy be the whisper of my name
If ever I were a wind about that tower
Or knew the way; but come with me," he said:
"I have a brother who has blown further than I."

"I might shriek till the world was small
As a turtle's egg; I have whipped my savagery
A pride of days beyond where the world ends
In burning, into the dark where no flames twitch,
Have blessed myself and hastily blown elsewhere,
But never glimpsed wrack nor wisp of that castle,
And whether there be any such place at all
I gravely doubt; but I have a brother
Wields the gale that flaps the chittering dead
Beyond where the world ends in ice; be sure
Unless his storm can shiver your conundrum
It is a thing unknown." The South Wind's wings
Howled, till they came to the door of the North Wind.

"Oh once," he roared, "I blew an aspen leaf
Beyond the glimmering world, over
The glass eaves of time, into that dark
Where no ice gleams; there, bristling, found that other
Wind of fear, but a rage stayed me until
The star-lashed sea, until I found the castle
That lies east of the sun and west of the moon.
But never I told a soul, for there I lay
Three weeks, frail as the aspen leaf, on the wild
Shore before I dared blow home again.
But if you be the lady that you claim,
Stay while I rest tonight and I shall try
Tomorrow if I can fly so far again."

Who has outflown the nightmare? Yet fast
Almost as she they flew in the morning
Beyond all boreal flickerings, headlong
Over the glass caves of time and found
The breathless dark where no souls stir,
But hair in another wind; broke, almost blind,
At last over a mad famished sea;
Then long as unspoken love they whirled.
But he wearied. The waves snapped at his knees,
The dog-toothed waves, till he whispered, "My wings fail,"
Sinking. But she cried, "I see a white shore,
A shadowy pinnacle that may be the castle
That lies east of the sun and west of the moon."

What if the breakers gulped and craved his thighs?
Where he had set her on the white shore
He fell forward and slept. Already
A foot beyond the frustrate sea there drowsed
Silence of forests, indolent, rimmed
With flutter of birches like birds in the tender
Sun, with thirsty osiers, pale hawthorn,
Perpetual apple trees, the capricious-limbed.
She saw in that light how the castle vanished
Above fancy among faithful clouds,
Saw the door, but nowhere near the door she went,
But sat under a guelder-rose and sang
"Ah, well-a-day," and played with the gold apple.

Till from an upper window of the castle
A princess with a nose three ells long
Called, "Who are you, singing 'well-a-day'
Under my window; and oh what will you take
And give me that golden apple?" "I am a lady
Of foreign ways singing to my own hair
A dirge for diminishing, under a pale tree,
Am a hazard waif blown from the scapegrace sea,
Am an aspen leaf; but nothing you own
Will I exchange for this gold apple,
Unless it should be that I might sleep tonight
Alone all night in his room with the prince
Who lives in this castle." And that could be arranged.

But she was returned, for earnest of gold,
Only a sleeping body and a sleep:
When she was led at evening into his room
Already he lay sleeping; for all she cried
His name aloud, for all she cried and kissed
His face and forehead, all night he lay sleeping.
What might she be but chorus to a dream,
But one who strokes a dream of chrysolite,
Glass pheasants, ducks ridiculous in stone,
A gold salmon in a beryl pool,
As reliquary, as meager communicance
Till daylight, then departs and sits again
By the tower and plays with the gold carding comb?

"Nothing whatever will I take," she said
When the princess called, "for my gold carding comb,
But to sleep tonight by the same prince."
But where was the unrecking fantasy,
The concord of distraught belief
She had named for love and understood by love,
If when she lay, and the second time, beside him
Nothing would answer to her kiss but sleep?
Must she before she wake still find a dream
Wherein she lay beside him, and he, waking,
Dreamed still of her? Although beside him, dream
Of yet more fortunate wakenings; till daylight;
Then sing by a gold spinning wheel, dreaming?

"I am a thirsty lady wishing I walked
Beside no water but a pool of beryl;
I sing to drown the silence of far flowers
And though I am deaf to all sounds other
Than a deafening heart in a distant room, I dream
I wander with my hands over my ears."
She argued with the princess as yesterday,
Parted with the gold spinning wheel. Oh must
Love's many mansions, the patient honeycomb
Of hope unlearn their heavens and at a sleep
Triply be consigned to cerements,
Or must salvation shrink to the unlikely
Monstrance of another's wakening?

Suppose the requisite vigil. Say one lay
Two nights awake beside the prince's room,
Heard crying there, as toward a vanishing spectre,
Told the prince, and he, thus wise against potions
The third night, sleepless, with wide arms received her,
Calling, "Oh love, is blessedness a risk
So delicate in time, that it should be
Tonight you find me? Tomorrow, always tomorrow
It is that my stepmother was to prevail,
It is that I was to marry that other princess.
But we are the sense of dawn beneath pretence
Of an order of darkness. Now lie in wisdom, mindful
Only of love, and leave to me tomorrow."

In the morning, to proud stepdame and coy princess,
"Call me a wry intransigent, a glass
Of fickle weathers, but what care I," he said,
"For decorum, though it be my wedding day?
Shall I be yoked to an unproven woman?
But who she may be can wash this shirt of mine,
Stained with three drops of tallow, white again
As once it was, she and no other lady
Will I marry. All wet the hands who wish;
All beat the board; all wring the linen; all wash
In the one water." Howsoever the princess
Dripped and wrung, the stains ran gray; or stepdame
Scrubbed, the shirt grew black as knavery.

"There is a girl outside the castle door,"
One said who loitered there and watched; "perhaps
She if she tried might wash it white again."
But vexed stepdame and angry princess
Raged then and screamed, "No no! Shall we have a tattered
Waif with outlandish ways for rival, and we
With our royal hands in water?" Yet the prince
Answered, "Let her come in, whoever she be."
She dipped the linen and once drew it forth
White as a leper; drew it forth again
White as blown snow; a third time raised it
Spotless, white as the violent moon; she said,
"How should I not, since all pallor is mine?"

The moon was musing in her high chamber
Among nine thousand mirrors. "Oh what am I,"
She cried, "but a trick of light, and tropically?
I walk in a wild charactry of night,
In a game of darkness figurative with tapers,
Toying with apples, and come upon myself
More often than is meet for sanity.
Oh, who would be shown, save in analogy,
—What for gold handsels and marvelous equerry—
As three hags sitting under an apple tree?
But I walk multifarious among
My baubles and horses; unless I go in a mask
How shall I know myself among my faces?"

"All metaphor," she said, "is magic. Let
Me be diverted in a turning lantern,
Let me in that variety be real.
But let the story be an improvisation
Continually, and through all repetition
Differ a little from itself, as though
Mistaken; and I a lady with foreign ways
To sing therein to my own hair." To the sun,
"You who tomorrow are my Pentecost,
Come dance with me—oh but be white, be wintry;
Oh lest I fall an utter prey to mirrors,
Be a white bear," she said "and come a-walking,
And ask my hand. I am a peasant's daughter."

Is it for nothing that a troupe of days
Makes repeated and perpetual rummage
In the lavish vestry; or should sun and moon,
Find mortality too mysterious,
Naked and with no guise but its own,
—Unless one of immortal gesture come
And by a mask should show it probable—
Believe a man, but not believe his story?
Say the year is the year of the phoenix.
Now, even now, over the rock hill
The tropical, the lucid moon, turning
Her mortal guises in the eye of a man,
Creates the image in which the world is.

COLLOQUY AT PENIEL

Countenance like lightning, why do you stand
In ebony raiment after no invocation
Suddenly where I knew no face, as though
You had stood so forever?

                —Say that the light
That is today, after so long becomes me,
Or that love's pleading incense that rose once
For mercy pleads now no longer, whereupon
The air conceives new clarity, and there
Suddenly I am visible. But know
I was the urgency that framed that love
And made it cry for mercy, the question
And the voice of the woman whispering, "Be content,
Be content."

        I am that which you lost
Behind you which you seek before you, for I
Am certain: sullen under your gaiety
And still its root and entrepreneur; footloose,
Not musical, but moving in all your music,
Assumed in all apostrophes.

                Think of me
As of a dusk through which no herds go home,
Quiet, perhaps, yet inexcusably
Disquieting, with a voice of infinite patience,
Gentle until resisted, like sheep bells
In the next valley.

          And I am he
With whom on a desperate hill, because I was
The closest combatant, always last night
You wrestled, as with the angel of your dark,
And overcame, yet in defeat who found
Such re-creation, always I rose with dawn
Enlarged by falling, as though I were the angel,
Equally, of your day. Yet one day
—Heaven and hills having endured—your arm,
Hopeless long since of conquest, will strike upon
Fatal surprise and end me there; and through
The evening slanting always at hand among
Unstartled trees, under a world of birds
Settling like dust despite the clang of triumph,
It will be your body that will fall.

From Green With Beasts *1956*

LEVIATHAN

This is the black sea-brute bulling through wave-wrack,
Ancient as ocean's shifting hills, who in sea-toils
Travelling, who furrowing the salt acres
Heavily, his wake hoary behind him,
Shoulders spouting, the fist of his forehead
Over wastes gray-green crashing, among horses unbroken
From bellowing fields, past bone-wreck of vessels,
Tide-ruin, wash of lost bodies bobbing
No longer sought for, and islands of ice gleaming,
Who ravening the rank flood, wave-marshalling,
Overmastering the dark sea-marches, finds home
And harvest. Frightening to foolhardiest
Mariners, his size were difficult to describe:
The hulk of him is like hills heaving,
Dark, yet as crags of drift-ice, crowns cracking in thunder,
Like land's self by night black-looming, surf churning and trailing
Along his shores' rushing, shoal-water boding
About the dark of his jaws; and who should moor at his edge
And fare on afoot would find gates of no gardens,
But the hill of dark underfoot diving,
Closing overhead, the cold deep, and drowning.
He is called Leviathan, and named for rolling,
First created he was of all creatures,
He has held Jonah three days and nights,
He is that curling serpent that in ocean is,
Sea-fright he is, and the shadow under the earth.
Days there are, nonetheless, when he lies
Like an angel, although a lost angel
On the waste's unease, no eye of man moving,
Bird hovering, fish flashing, creature whatever
Who after him came to herit earth's emptiness.
Froth at flanks seething soothes to stillness,
Waits; with one eye he watches
Dark of night sinking last, with one eye dayrise
As at first over foaming pastures. He makes no cry
Though that light is a breath. The sea curling,
Star-climbed, wind-combed, cumbered with itself still
As at first it was, is the hand not yet contented
Of the Creator. And he waits for the world to begin.

THE BATHERS

They make in the twining tide the motions of birds.
Such are the cries, also, they exchange
In their nakedness that is soft as a bird's
Held in the hand, and as fragile and strange.

And the blue mirror entertains them till they take
The sea for another bird: the crumbling
Hush-hush where the gentlest of waves break
About their voices would be his bright feathers blowing.

Only the dull shore refrains. But from this patient
Bird each, in the plumage of his choice,
Might learn the deep shapes and secret of flight

And the shore be merely a perch to which they might
Return. And the mirror turns serpent
And their only sun is swallowed up like a voice.

THE WILDERNESS

Remoteness is its own secret. Not holiness,
Though, nor the huge spirit miraculously avoiding
The way's dissemblings, and undue distraction or drowning
At the watercourses, has found us this place,

But merely surviving all that is not here,
Till the moment that looks up, almost by chance, and sees
Perhaps hands, feet, but not ourselves; a few stunted juniper trees
And the horizon's virginity. We are where we always were.

The secret becomes no less itself for our presence
In the midst of it; as the lizard's gold-eyed
Mystery is no more lucid for being near.

And famine is all about us, but not here;
For from the very hunger to look, we feed
Unawares, as at the beaks of ravens.

THE WAKENING

Looking up at last from the first sleep
Of necessity rather than of pure delight
While his dreams still rode and lapped like the morning light
That everywhere in the world shimmered and lay deep

So that his sight was half dimmed with its dazzling, he could see
Her standing naked in the day-shallows there,
Face turned away, hands lost in her bright hair;
And he saw then that her shadow was the tree:

For in a place where he could never come
Only its darkness underlay the day's splendor,
So that even as she stood there it must reach down

Through not roots but branches with dark bird-song, into a stream
Of silence like a sky but deeper
Than this light or than any remembered heaven.

THE MOUNTAIN

Only on the rarest occasions, when the blue air,
Though clear, is not too blinding (as, say,
For a particular moment just at dusk in autumn)
Or if the clouds should part suddenly
Between freshets in spring, can one trace the rising
Slopes high enough to call them contours; and even
More rarely see above the treeline. Then
It is with almost a shock that one recognizes
What supposedly one had known always:
That it is, in fact, a mountain; not merely
This restrictive sense of nothing level, of never
Being able to go anywhere
But up or down, until it seems probable
Sometimes that the slope, to be so elusive
And yet so inescapable, must be nothing
But ourselves: that we have grown with one
Foot shorter than the other, and would deform
The levellest habitat to our misshapen
Condition, as is said of certain hill creatures.

Standing between two other peaks, but not
As they: or so we have seen in a picture
Whose naive audacity, founded as far as can be
Determined, on nothing but the needs
Of its own composition, presents all three
As shaped oddly, of different colours, rising
From a plain whose flatness appears incredible
To such as we. Of course to each of us
Privately, its chief difference from its peers
Rests not even in its centrality, but its
Strangeness composed of our own intimacy
With a part of it, our necessary
Ignorance of its limits, and diurnal pretence
That what we see of it is all. Learned opinions differ
As to whether it was ever actively
Volcanic. It is believed that if one could see it
Whole, its shape might make this clearer, but that
Is impossible, for at the distance at which in theory
One could see it all, it would be out of sight.

Of course in all the senses in which any
Place or thing can be said not to exist
Until someone, at least, is known to have been there,
It would help immeasurably if anyone
Should ever manage to climb it. No one,
From whatever distance, has ever so much as seen
The summit, or even anywhere near it; not, that is,
As far as we know. At one time the attempt
Was a kind of holy maelstrom, Mecca
For fanatics and madmen, and a mode of ritual
And profane suicide (since among us there is nowhere
From which one could throw oneself down). But there have been
Expeditions even quite recently, and with the benefit
Of the most expensive equipment. Very few
Who set out at all seriously have
Come back. At a relatively slight distance
Above us, apparently the whole aspect and condition
Of the mountain changes completely; there is ceaseless wind
With a noise like thunder and the beating of wings.

Indeed, if one considers the proximity
Of the point at which so much violence
Is known to begin, it is not our failure
That strikes one as surprising, but our impunity:
The summer camps on near gradients, ski-lifts in winter,
And even our presence where we are. For of those
Who attained any distance and returned, most
Were deafened, some permanently; some were blind,
And these also often incurably; all
Without exception were dazzled, as by a great light. And those
Who perhaps went furthest and came back, seemed
To have completely lost the use of our language,
Or if they spoke, babbled incoherently
Of silence bursting beyond that clamour, of time
Passed there not passing here, which we could not understand,
Of time no time at all. These characteristic
Effects of the upper slopes—especially the derangement
Of time-sense, and the dazzling—seem from earliest
Antiquity to have excited speculation.

One legend has it that a remote king-priest figure
Once gained the summit, spent some—to him non-sequent
But to them significant—time there, and returned
"Shining," bearing ciphers of the arcane (which,
Translated into the common parlance, proved
To be a list of tribal taboos) like clastic
Specimens, and behaved with a glacial violence
Later construed as wisdom. This, though
Charming, does not, in the light of current endeavour,
Seem possible, even though so long ago. Yet
To corroborate this story, in the torrent
Gold has been found which even at this
Late date appears to have been powdered by hand,
And (further to confuse inquiry) several
Pediments besides, each with four sockets shaped
As though to receive the hoof of a giant statue
Of some two-toed ungulate. Legend being
What it is, there are those who still insist
He will come down again some day from the mountain.

As there are those who say it will fall on us. It
Will fall. And those who say it has already
Fallen. It has already fallen. Have we not
Seen it fall in shadow, evening after evening,
Across everything we can touch; do we not build
Our houses out of the great hard monoliths
That have crashed down from far above us? Shadows
Are not without substance, remind and predict;
And we know we live between greater commotions
Than any we can describe. But, most important:
Since this, though we know so little of it, is
All we know, is it not whatever it makes us
Believe of it—even the old woman
Who laughs, pointing, and says that the clouds across
Its face are wings of seraphim? Even the young
Man who, standing on it, declares it is not
There at all. He stands with one leg habitually
Bent, to keep from falling, as though he had grown
That way, as is said of certain hill creatures.

SAINT SEBASTIAN

So many times I have felt them come, Lord,
The arrows (a coward dies often), so many times,
And worse, oh worse often than this. Neither breeze nor bird
Stirring the hazed peace through which the day climbs.

And slower even than the arrows, the few sounds that come
Falling, as across water, from where farther off than the hills
The archers move in a different world in the same
Kingdom. Oh, can the noise of angels,

The beat and whirring between Thy kingdoms
Be even by such cropped feathers raised? Not though
With the wings of the morning may I fly from Thee; for it is

Thy kingdom where (and the wind so still now)
I stand in pain; and, entered with pain as always,
Thy kingdom that on these erring shafts comes.

THE STATION

Two boards with a token roof, backed
Against the shelving hill, and a curtain
Of frayed sacking which the wind absently
Toyed with on the side toward the sea:
From that point already so remote that we
Continually caught ourselves talking in whispers
No path went on but only the still country
Unfolding as far as we could see
In the luminous dusk its land that had not been lived on
Ever, or not within living memory.

This less than shelter, then, was the last
Human contrivance for our encouragement:
Improvised so hastily, it might have been
Thrown together only the moment
Before we arrived, yet so weathered,
Warped and parched, it must have stood there
Longer than we knew. And the ground before it
Was not scarred with the rawness of construction
Nor even beaten down by feet, but simply barren
As one felt it always had been: something between
Sand and red shale with only the spiky dune-grass
Growing, and a few trees stunted by wind.

Some as they arrived appeared to be carrying
Whole households strapped onto their shoulders,
Often with their tired children asleep
Among the upper baskets, and even
A sore dog limping behind them. Some
Were travelling light for the journey:
A knife and matches, and would sleep
In the clothes they stood up in. And there were
The barefoot ones, some from conviction
With staves, some from poverty with nothing.

Burdens and garments bore no relation
To the ages of the travellers; nor, as they sat
In spite of fatigue talking late
Into the night, to the scope and firmness
Of their intentions. It was, for example,
A patriarch herding six grandchildren
In his family, and who had carried

More than his own weight of gear all day
Who insisted that three days' journey inland
Would bring them to a sheltered valley
Along a slow river, where even the clumsiest farmer
Would grow fat on the land's three crops a year.

And a youth with expensive hiking shoes
And one blanket to carry, who declaimed
Most loudly on the effort of the trip,
The stingy prospects, the risks involved
In venturing beyond that point. Several
Who had intended to go furthest mused
That the land thereabouts was better
Than what they had left and that tramping
Behind his own plough should be far enough afield
For any grown man, while another, to all
Dissuasions repeated that it had been
The same ten years ago at—naming a place
Where we had slept two nights before.
Until one who looked most energetic
Changed the subject with his theory
That a certain block of stone there
Before the doorway had been shaped
By hand, and at one time had stood
As the pedestal of a wayside shrine.

Yet in spite of the circling arguments
Which grew desperate several times before morning
Everyone knew that it was all decided:
That some, even who spoke with most eloquence
Of the glories of exodus and the country
Waiting to be taken, would be found
Scrabbling next day for the patch of ground
Nearest the shelter, or sneaking back
The way they had come, or hiring themselves out
As guides to this point, and no one would be able
To explain what had stopped them there; any more
Than one would be able afterwards to say
Why some who perhaps sat there saying least,
And not, to appearances, the bravest
Or best suited for such a journey,
At first light would get up and go on.

THE MASTER

Not entirely enviable, however envied;
And early outgrew the enjoyment of their envy,
For other preoccupations, some quite as absurd.
Not always edifying in his action: touchy
And dull by turns, prejudiced, often not strictly
Truthful, with a weakness for petty meddling,
For black sheep, churlish rancours, and out-of-hand damning.

The messes he got himself into were of his own devising.
He had all the faults he saw through in the rest of us,
As we have taken pains, and a certain delight, in proving,
Not denying his strength, but still not sure quite where it was;
But luck was with him too, whatever that is,
For his rightful deserts, far from destroying him,
Turned out to be just what he'd needed, and he used them.

Opportunist, shrewd waster, half calculation,
Half difficult child; a phoney, it would seem
Even to his despairs, were it not for the work, and that certain
Sporadic but frightening honesty allowed him
By those who loathed him most. Not nice in the home,
But a few loved him. And he loved. Who? What? Some still
Think they know, as some thought they knew then, which is just as well.

In his lifetime what most astonished those
Acquainted with him, was the amount of common
Detail he could muster, and with what intimate ease,
As though he knew it all from inside. For when
Had he seen it? They recalled him as one who most often
Seemed slow, even stupid, not above such things surely,
But absent, with that air maybe part fake, and part shifty.

Yet famously cursed in his disciples:
So many, emulous, but without his unique powers,
Could only ape and exaggerate his foibles.
And he bewildered them as he did no others,
Though they tried to conceal it: for, like mirrors
In a fun-house, they were static, could never keep up with him,
Let alone predict. But stranded on strange shores following him.

So the relief, then the wide despair, when he was gone;
For not only his imitators did he leave feeling
Naked, without voice or manner of their own:

For over a generation his ghost would come bullying
Every hand: all modes seemed exhausted, and he had left nothing
Of any importance for them to do,
While what had escaped him eluded them also.

For only with his eyes could they see, with his ears hear
The world. He had made it. And hard, now, to believe
In the invention: all seems so styleless, as though it had come there
By itself, since the errors and effort are in their grave.
But real: here we are walking in it. Oh what we can never forgive
Is the way every leaf calls up to our helpless remembrance
Our reality and its insupportable innocence.

LEARNING A DEAD LANGUAGE

There is nothing for you to say. You must
Learn first to listen. Because it is dead
It will not come to you of itself, nor would you
Of yourself master it. You must therefore
Learn to be still when it is imparted,
And, though you may not yet understand, to remember.

What you remember is saved. To understand
The least thing fully you would have to perceive
The whole grammar in all its accidence
And all its system, in the perfect singleness
Of intention it has because it is dead.
You can learn only a part at a time.

What you are given to remember
Has been saved before you from death's dullness by
Remembering. The unique intention
Of a language whose speech has died is order
Incomplete only where someone has forgotten.
You will find that that order helps you to remember.

What you come to remember becomes yourself.
Learning will be to cultivate the awareness
Of that governing order, now pure of the passions
It composed; till, seeking it in itself,
You may find at last the passion that composed it,
Hear it both in its speech and in yourself.

What you remember saves you. To remember
Is not to rehearse, but to hear what never
Has fallen silent. So your learning is,
From the dead, order, and what sense of yourself
Is memorable, what passion may be heard
When there is nothing for you to say.

LOW FIELDS AND LIGHT

I think it is in Virginia, that place
That lies across the eye of my mind now
Like a grey blade set to the moon's roundness,
Like a plain of glass touching all there is.

The flat fields run out to the sea there.
There is no sand, no line. It is autumn.
The bare fields, dark between fences, run
Out to the idle gleam of the flat water.

And the fences go on out, sinking slowly,
With a cow-bird half-way, on a stunted post, watching
How the light slides through them easy as weeds
Or wind, slides over them away out near the sky.

Because even a bird can remember
The fields that were there before the slow
Spread and wash of the edging light crawled
There and covered them, a little more each year.

My father never plowed there, nor my mother
Waited, and never knowingly I stood there
Hearing the seepage slow as growth, nor knew
When the taste of salt took over the ground.

But you would think the fields were something
To me, so long I stare out, looking
For their shapes or shadows through the matted gleam, seeing
Neither what is nor what was, but the flat light rising.

TWO PAINTINGS BY ALFRED WALLIS

i
Voyage to Labrador

Tonight when the sea runs like a sore,
Swollen as hay and with the same sound,
Where under the hat-dark the iron
Ship slides seething, hull crammed
With clamors the fluttering hues of a fever,
Clang-battened in, the stunned bells done
From the rung-down quartans, and only
The dotty lights still trimmed
Abroad like teeth, there dog-hunched will the high
Street of hugging bergs have come
To lean huge and hidden as women,
Untouched as smoke and, at our passing, pleased
Down to the private sinks of their cold.
Then we will be white, all white, as cloths sheening,
Stiff as teeth, white as the sticks
And eyes of the blind. But morning, mindless
And uncaring as Jesus, will find nothing
In that same place but an empty sea
Colorless, see, as a glass of water.

ii
Schooner Under the Moon

Waits where we would almost be. Part
Pink as a tongue; floats high on the olive
Rumpled night-flood, foresails and clouds hiding
Such threat and beauty as we may never see.

THE SHIPWRECK

The tale is different if even a single breath
Escapes to tell it. The return itself
Says survival is possible. And words made to carry
In quiet the burden, the isolation
Of dust, and that fail even so,
Though they shudder still, must shrink the great head
Of elemental violence, the vast eyes
Called blind looking into the ends of darkness,
The mouth deafening understanding with its one
All-wise syllable, into a shrivelled
History that the dry-shod may hold
In the palms of their hands. They had her
Under jib and reefed mizzen, and in the dark
Were fairly sure where they were, and with sea-room,
And it seemed to be slacking a little, until
Just before three they struck. Heard
It come home, hollow in the hearts of them,
And only then heard the bell ringing, telling them
It had been ringing there always telling them
That there it would strike home, hollow, in
The hearts of them. Only then heard it
Over the sunlight, the dozing creak
Of the moorings, the bleaching quay, the heat,
The coiled ropes on the quay the day they would sail
And the day before, and across the water blue
As a sky through the heat beyond
The coils, the coils, with their shadows coiled
Inside them. And it sprang upon them dark,
Bitter, and heavy with sound. They began to go
To pieces at once under the waves' hammer.
Sick at heart since that first stroke, they moved
Nevertheless as they had learned always to move
When it should come, not weighing hope against
The weight of the water, yet knowing that no breath
Would escape to betray what they underwent then.
Dazed too, incredulous, that it had come,
That they could recognize it. It was too familiar,
And they in the press of it, therefore, as though
In a drifting dream. But it bore in upon them
Bursting slowly inside them where they had
Coiled it down, coiled it down: this sea, it was
Blind, yes, as they had said, and treacherous—

They had used their own traits to character it—but without
Accident in its wildness, in its rage,
Utterly and from the beginning without
Error. And to some it seemed that the waves
Grew gentle, spared them, while they died of that knowledge.

THE EYES OF THE DROWNED WATCH KEELS GOING OVER

Where the light has no horizons we lie.
It dims into depth not distance. It sways
Like hair, then we shift and turn over slightly.
As once on the long swing under the trees
In the drowse of summer we slid to and fro
Slowly in the soft wash of the air, looking
Upwards through the leaves that turned over and back
Like hands, through the birds, the fathomless light,
Upwards. They go over us swinging
Jaggedly, labouring between our eyes
And the light. Churning their wrought courses
Between the sailing birds and the awed eyes
Of the fish, with the grace of neither, nor with
The stars' serenity that they follow.
Yet the light shakes around them as they go.
Why? And why should we, rocking on shoal-pillow,
With our eyes cling to them, and their wakes follow,
Who follow nothing? If we could remember
The stars in their clarity, we might understand now
Why we pursued stars, to what end our eyes
Fastened upon stars, how it was that we traced
In their remote courses not their own fates but ours.

From The Drunk in the Furnace
1960

ODYSSEUS

Always the setting forth was the same,
Same sea, same dangers waiting for him
As though he had got nowhere but older.
Behind him on the receding shore
The identical reproaches, and somewhere
Out before him, the unravelling patience
He was wedded to. There were the islands
Each with its woman and twining welcome
To be navigated, and one to call "home."
The knowledge of all that he betrayed
Grew till it was the same whether he stayed
Or went. Therefore he went. And what wonder
If sometimes he could not remember
Which was the one who wished on his departure
Perils that he could never sail through,
And which, improbable, remote, and true,
Was the one he kept sailing home to?

THE ICEBERG

It is not its air but our own awe
That freezes us. Hardest of all to believe
That so fearsome a destroyer can be
Dead, with those lights moving in it,
With the sea all around it charged
With its influence. It seems that only now
We realize the depth of the waters, the
Abyss over which we float among such
Clouds. And still not understanding
The coldness of most elegance, even
With so vast and heartless a splendor
Before us, stare, caught in the magnetism
Of great silence, thinking: this is the terror
That cannot be charted, this is only
A little of it. And recall how many
Mariners, watching the sun set, have seen
These peaks on the horizon and made sail
Through the darkness for islands that no map
Had promised, floating blessèd in
The west. These must dissolve
Before they can again grow apple trees.

FOG-HORN

Surely that moan is not the thing
That men thought they were making, when they
Put it there, for their own necessities.
That throat does not call to anything human
But to something men had forgotten,
That stirs under fog. Who wounded that beast
Incurably, or from whose pasture
Was it lost, full grown, and time closed round it
With no way back? Who tethered its tongue
So that its voice could never come
To speak out in the light of clear day,
But only when the shifting blindness
Descends and is acknowledged among us,
As though from under a floor it is heard,
Or as though from behind a wall, always
Nearer than we had remembered? If it
Was we that gave tongue to this cry
What does it bespeak in us, repeating
And repeating, insisting on something
That we never meant? We only put it there
To give warning of something we dare not
Ignore, lest we should come upon it
Too suddenly, recognize it too late,
As our cries were swallowed up and all hands lost.

DECEPTION ISLAND

You can go farther. The south itself
Goes much farther, hundreds of miles, first
By sea, then over the white continent,
Mountainous, unmapped, all the way to the pole.

But sometimes imagination
Is content to rest here, at harbor
In the smooth bay in the dead mountain,
Like a vessel at anchor in its own reflection.

The glassy roadstead sleeps in a wide ring
Of ice and igneous shingle, whose gradual
Slopes rise, under streaks of white and black all
The swept shapes of wind, to the volcano's ridges.

It is like being suspended in the open
Vast wreck of a stony skull dead for ages.
You cannot believe the crater was ever
Fiery, before it filled with silence, and sea.

It is not a place you would fancy
You would like to go to. The slopes are barren
Of all the vegetation of desire.
But a place to imagine lying at anchor,

Watching the sea outside the broken
Temple of the cold fire-head, and wondering
Less at the wastes of silence and distance
Than at what all that lonely fire was for.

THE PORTLAND GOING OUT

Early that afternoon, as we keep
Remembering, the water of the harbor
Was so smooth you wanted to walk on it,
It looked that trustworthy: glassy and black
Like one of those pools they have in the lobbies
Of grand hotels. And, thinking back, we say
That the same bells we had heard telling
Their shoals and hours since we were children,
Sounded different, as though they were
Moving about the business of strangers. By
Five it was kicking up quite a bit,
And the greasiest evening you ever saw;
We had just come in, and were making fast,
A few minutes to seven, when she went
Down the harbor behind us, going out,
Passing so close over our stern that we
Caught the red glow of her port light for
A moment on our faces. Only
When she was gone did we notice
That it was starting to snow. No, we were
Not the last, nor even nearly the last
To see her. A schooner that lived through it
Glimpsed her, at the height of the storm,
In a clear patch, apparently riding it;
That must have been no more than minutes
Before she went down. We had known storms
Before, almost as brutal, and wrecks before
Almost as unexplained, almost
As disastrous. Yet we keep asking
How it happened, how, and why Blanchard sailed,
Miscalculating the storm's course. But what
We cannot even find questions for
Is how near we were: brushed by the same snow,
Lifted by her wake as she passed. We could
Have spoken, we swear, with anyone on her deck,
And not had to raise our voices, if we
Had known anything to say. And now
In no time at all, she has put
All of disaster between us: a gulf
Beyond reckoning, It begins where we are.

FABLE

However the man had got himself there,
There he clung, kicking in mid-air,
Hanging from the top branch of a high tree
With his grip weakening gradually.
A passer-by who noticed him
Moved a safe distance from under the limb,
And then stood with his arms akimbo, calling,
"Let go, or you'll be killed; the tree is falling."
The man up on the branch, blindly clinging,
With his face toward heaven, and his knees heaving,
Heard this, through his depending to and fro,
And with his last ounce of good faith, let go.
No creature could have survived that fall,
And the stranger was not surprised at all
To find him dead, but told his body, "You
Only let go because you wanted to;
All you lacked was a good reason.
I let you hope you might save your skin
By taking the most comfortable way."
Then added, smiling, as he walked away,
"Besides, you'd have fallen anyway."

UNDER THE OLD ONE

Helpless improver,
Grown numerous and clever
Rather than wise or loving,
Nothing is newer than ever
Under the sun:

Still specious, wanton, venal,
Your noises as dull
And smiles self-flattering
As was usual
Under any heaven.

How often, before this,
You went on knees
To moons of your own making,
Abject, with no peace
Under the old one.

NO ONE

Who would it surprise
If (after the flash, hush, rush,
Thump and crumpling) when the wind of prophecy
Lifts its pitch, and over the drifting ash
At last the trump splits the sky,
No One should arise

(No one just as before:
No limbs, eyes, presence;
Mindless and incorruptible) to inherit
Without question the opening heavens,
To be alone, to be complete,
And so forever?

Who had kept our secrets,
Whose wisdom we had heeded,
Who had stood near us (we proved it) again
And again in the dark, to whom we had prayed
Naturally and most often,
Who had escaped our malice—

No more than equitable
By No One to be succeeded,
Who had known our merits, had believed
Our lies, before ourselves whom we had considered
And (after ourselves) had loved
Constantly and well.

PLEA FOR A CAPTIVE

Woman with the caught fox
By the scruff, you can drop your hopes:
It will not tame though you prove kind,
Though you entice it with fat ducks
Patiently to your fingertips
And in dulcet love enclose it
Do not suppose it will turn friend,
Dog your heels, sleep at your feet,
Be happy in the house,
                              No,

It will only trot to and fro,
To and fro, with vacant eye,
Neither will its pelt improve
Nor its disposition, twisting
The raw song of its debasement
Through the long nights, and in your love,
In your delicate meats tasting
Nothing but its own decay
(As at first hand I have learned)
                              Oh

Kill it at once or let it go.

CHOICE OF PRIDES

To tell the truth, it would have its points
(Since fall we must) to do it proud:
To ride for your fall on a good mount
Hung with honors and looped garlands,
Moved by the crowd's flattering sounds,
Or to advance with brash din, banners,
Flights of arrows leaping like hounds.

But from a choice of prides I would pick
(Or so I hope) the bare cheek
To amble out, innocent of arms
And alone, under the cocked guns
Or what missiles might be in season,
And this in the pure brass of the act
Attired, and in no other armor.

Considering that, of every species
(I should reason) mine is most naked,
For all its draperies enacting
As a pink beast its honest nature,
I will take in this raw condition
What pride I can, not have my boast
In glad-rags, my bravery plated.

And I should think myself twice lucky
(Stuck with my choice) if I could be sure
That I had been egged on by nothing
But neat pride, and not (as is common,)
Brought to it by the veiled promptings
Of vanity, or by poverty
Or the fecklessness of despair.

BLIND GIRL

     Silent, with her eyes
Climbing above her like a pair of hands drowning,
Up the tower stairs she runs headlong, turning
In a spiral of voices that grow no fainter, though
At each turn, through the tiny window,
The blood-shrieking starlings, flaking into the trees,
     Sound farther below.

     Still, as she runs
Turn above turn round the hollow flights, so
Ringing higher, the towering voices follow,
Out of each room renewed as she passes,
To echo, hopeless: their shrieked entreaties
Singing their love, and their gross resonance
     Her beauty's praises,

     With no name too tender,
High, or childish to din their desperate
Invocations; confessing; swearing to dedicate
Their split hearts on salvers if only she
Will pause. Each raw plea raucous less to delay,
At last, than to claim her: "Though you turn for no other,
     Dear soul, this is me, me!"

     But buffeted and stunned
By their spun cries as in clambering water,
Now if she tried she could not remember
Which door among those, nor what care, crime,
Possession, name, she had bolted from,
Nor how, the way opening to her blind hand,
     She had slipped past them,

     Nor how many centuries
Ago. Only tells herself over and over
That their winding calls cannot forever
Build, but at their shrill peak stairs, tower, all
Into the loose air sprung suddenly, will fall,
Breathless, to nothing, and instantly her repose
     Be silent and final.

ONE-EYE

("In the country of the blind the one-eyed man is king.")

On that vacant day
After kicking and moseying here and there
For some time, he lifted that carpet-corner
    His one eye-lid, and the dyed light
Leapt at him from all sides like dogs. Also hues
That he had never heard of, in that place
    Were bleeding and playing.

    Even so, it was
Only at the grazing of light fingers
Over his face, unannounced, and then his
    Sight of many mat eyes, paired white
Irises like dried peas looking, that it dawned
On him: his sidelong idling had found
    The country of the blind.

    Whose swarming digits
Knew him at once: their king, come to them
Out of a saying. And chanting an anthem
    Unto his one eye, to the dry
Accompaniment that their leaping fingers made
Flicking round him like locusts in a cloud,
    They took him home with them.

    Their shapely city
Shines like a suit. On a plain chair he was set
In a cloak of hands, and crowned, to intricate
    Music. They sent him their softest
Daughters, clad only in scent and their own
Vast ears, meantime making different noises
    In each ante-chamber.

    They can be wakened
Sometimes by a feather falling on the next
Floor, and they keep time by the water-clocks'
    Dropping even when they sleep. Once
He would expound to them all, from his only
Light, day breaking, the sky spiked and the
    Earth amuck with color,

And they would listen,
Amazed at his royalty, gaping like
Sockets, and would agree, agree, blank
    As pearls. At the beginning.
Alone in brightness, soon he spoke of it
In sleep only; "Look, look," he would call out
    In the dark only.

    Now in summer gaudy
With birds he says nothing; of their thefts, often
Beheld, and their beauties, now for a long time
    Nothing. Nothing, day after day,
To see the black thumb as big as a valley
Over their heads descending silently
    Out of a quiet sky.

SMALL WOMAN ON SWALLOW STREET

Four feet up, under the bruise-blue
Fingered hat-felt, the eyes begin. The sly brim
Slips over the sky, street after street, and nobody
Knows, to stop it. It will cover
The whole world, if there is time. Fifty years'
Start in gray the eyes have; you will never
Catch up to where they are, too clever
And always walking, the legs not long but
The boots big with wide smiles of darkness
Going round and round at their tops, climbing.
They are almost to the knees already, where
There should have been ankles to stop them.
So must keep walking all the time, hurry, for
The black sea is down where the toes are
And swallows and swallows all. A big coat
Can help save you. But eyes push you down; never
Meet eyes. There are hands in hands, and love
Follows its furs into shut doors; who
Shall be killed first? Do not look up there:
The wind is blowing the building-tops, and a hand
Is sneaking the whole sky another way, but
It will not escape. Do not look up. God is
On High. He can see you. You will die.

THE GLEANERS

They always gather on summer nights there
On the corner under the buggy street-bulb,
Chewing their dead stubs outside the peeling
      Bar, those foreign old men,

Till the last street-car has squealed and gone
An hour since into the growing silence,
Leaving only the bugs' sounds, and their own breathing;
      Sometime then they hobble off.

Some were already where they stay, last night,
In rooms, fumbling absently with laces,
Straps, trusses, one hand was nearly to a glass
      With a faceful of teeth

At the time the siren went shrieking for
The fire in the cigar factory there,
Half the town by then stinking like a crooked
      Stogie. Well there they are

Where all day they have been, beetling over
The charred pile, teetering like snails and careful
Under sooty hats, in ankle shoes, vests,
      Shirts grimed at collars and wrists,

Bending, babying peck baskets as they
Revolve on painful feet over the rubble,
Raking with crooked knuckles the amber pools
      For limp cheroots.

After dark there will still be a few turning
Slowly with flashlights. Except for coughs they are quiet;
Sober; they always knew something would happen,
      Something would provide.

POOL ROOM IN THE LIONS' CLUB

I'm sure it must be still the same,
Year after year, the faded room
Upstairs out of the afternoon,
The spidery hands, stalking and cautious
Round and round the airless light,
The few words like the dust settling
Across the quiet, the shadows waiting
Intent and still around the table
For the ivory click, the sleeves stirring,
Swirling the smoke, the hats circling
Remote and hazy above the light,
The board creaking, then hushed again.
Trains from the sea-board rattle past,
And from St. Louis and points west,
But nothing changes their concern,
Hurries or calls them. They must think
The whole world is nothing more
Than their gainless harmless pastime
Of utter patience protectively
Absorbed around one smooth table
Safe in its ring of dusty light
Where the real dark can never come.

JOHN OTTO

John Otto of Brunswick, ancestor
On my mother's side, Latin scholar,
Settler of the Cumberland Valley,
Schoolmaster, sire of a family,
Why, one day in your white age,
Did you heave up onto your old man's legs
In the house near Blain, in Perry County,
And shut the gate and shuffle away
From the home of eighty years or so
And what cronies were left, and follow
The road out of the valley, up the hill,
Over the south mountain, to Carlisle,
The whole way on foot, in the wagon tracks,
To die of fatigue there, at ninety-six?
I can see Carlisle Valley spread below
And you, John, coming over the hill's brow,
Stopping for breath and a long look;
I can hear your breath come sharp and quick,
But why it was that you climbed up there
None of us remembers any more.
To see your son and his family?
Was the house too quiet in Perry County?
To ask some question, tell some secret,
Or beg some pardon before too late?
Or was it to look once again
On another valley green in the sun
Almost as in the beginning, to remind
Your eyes of a promise in the land?

GRANDFATHER IN THE OLD MEN'S HOME

Gentle at last, and as clean as ever,
He did not even need drink any more,
And his good sons unbent and brought him
Tobacco to chew, both times when they came
To be satisfied he was well cared for.
And he smiled all the time to remember
Grandmother, his wife, wearing the true faith
Like an iron nightgown, yet brought to birth
Seven times and raising the family
Through her needle's eye while he got away
Down the green river, finding directions
For boats. And himself coming home sometimes
Well-heeled but blind drunk, to hide all the bread
And shoot holes in the bucket while he made
His daughters pump. Still smiled as kindly in
His sleep beside the other clean old men
To see Grandmother, every night the same,
Huge in her age, with her thumbed-down mouth, come
Hating the river, filling with her stare
His gliding dream, while he turned to water,
While the children they both had begotten,
With old faces now, but themselves shrunken
To child-size again, stood ranged at her side,
Beating their little Bibles till he died.

GRANDMOTHER WATCHING
AT HER WINDOW

There was always the river or the train
Right past the door, and someone might be gone
Come morning. When I was a child I mind
Being held up at a gate to wave
Good-bye, good-bye to I didn't know who,
Gone to the War, and how I cried after.
When I married I did what was right
But I knew even that first night
That he would go. And so shut my soul tight
Behind my mouth, so he could not steal it
When he went. I brought the children up clean
With my needle, taught them that stealing
Is the worst sin; knew if I loved them
They would be taken away, and did my best
But must have loved them anyway
For they slipped through my fingers like stitches.
Because God loves us always, whatever
We do. You can sit all your life in churches
And teach your hands to clutch when you pray
And never weaken, but God loves you so dearly
Just as you are, that nothing you are can stay,
But all the time you keep going away, away.

GRANDMOTHER DYING

Not ridden in her Christian bed, either,
But her wrenched back bent double, hunched over
The plank tied to the arms of her rocker
With a pillow on it to keep her head
Sideways up from her knees, and three others
Behind her in the high chair to hold her
Down so the crooked might be straight, as if
There was any hope. Who for ninety-three years,
Keeping the faith, believed you could get
Through the strait gate and the needle's eye if
You made up your mind straight and narrow, kept
The thread tight and, dead both to left and to right
To the sly music beyond the ditches, beat
Time on the book as you went. And then she fell.
She should have did what she was told, she should
Have called for what she needed, she did look
Sleeping on the pillows and to be trusted
Just for a bit, and Bid was not downstairs
A minute before hearing the hall creak
And the door crash back in the bathroom as
She fell. What was it, eighteen months, they took
Care of her crooked that way, feeding from
The side, hunching down to hear her, all
Knowing full well what the crooked come to
When their rockers stop. Still could hear what she
Thought good to hear, still croak: you keep my
Candy hid in that sweater drawer, Bid,
Only for company one piece, then you put it
Back again, hear? One after the other
A family of fevers visited her,
And last a daughter-in-law with a nasty
Cough combed her hair out pretty on the plank,
With a flower in it, and held a mirror
For her to see till it made her smile, but
Bid, she whispered, you keep wide of that new
Nurse's cough, she has T.B. And where
Were the wars that still worried her, when
Most were dead a long time ago, and one
Son had come back and was there hanging
In sunlight, in a medal of glory, on
The wall in her room smelling of coal-gas
And petunias. One daughter lived and dusted

A nice brick house a block away, already
Rehearsing how she'd say, "Well, we was always
Good to our Mumma anyway." Outside,
The crooked river flowed easy, knowing
All along; the tracks smiled and rang away;
Help would come from the hills. One knotted hand
Of hers would hang up in the air above
Her head for hours, propped on its elbow, waving
In that direction. And when she heaved up
Her last breath, to shake it like a fist,
As out of a habit so old as to be
Nearly absent, at the dirty river
Sliding away there the same as ever,
Bid says you could not hear her because there
Came a black engine that had been waiting
Up the tracks there for ninety-four years, and
Snatched it out from her lips, and roared off
With it hooting downriver, making the tracks
Straighten out in front of it like a whip,
While the windows rattled loud to break, the things
On the shelves shook, the folds of her face jarred
And shivered; and when it was gone, for a long
Time the goosed laundry still leaped and jiggled
In the smutty wind outside, and her chair went on
Rocking all by itself with nothing alive
Inside it to explain it, nothing, nothing.

THE NATIVE

He and his, unwashed all winter,
In that abandoned land in the punished
North, in a gnashing house sunk as a cheek,
Nest together, a bunting bundle crumpled
Like a handkerchief on the croaking
Back-broken bed jacked up in the kitchen; the clock
Soon stops, they just keep the cooker going; all
Kin to begin with when they crawl in under,
      Who covers who they don't care.

He and his, in the settled cozy,
Steam like a kettle, rock-a-bye, the best
Went west long ago, got out from under,
Waved bye-bye to the steep scratched fields and scabby
Pastures: their chapped plaster of newspapers
Still chafes from the walls, and snags of string tattling
Of their rugs trail yet from stair-nails. The rest,
Never the loftiest, left to themselves,
      Descended, descended.

Most that's his, at the best of times,
Looks about to fall: the propped porch lurches
Through a herd of licked machines crutched in their last
Seizures, each as ominously leaning
As the framed ancestors, trapped in their collars,
Beetling out of oval clouds from the black
Tops of the rooms, their unappeasable jowls
By nothing but frayed, faded cords leashed
      To the leaking walls.

But they no more crash
Onto him and his than the cobwebs, or
The gritting rafters, though on the summer-people's
Solid houses the new-nailed shingles open
All over like doors, flap, decamp, the locked
Shutters peel wide to wag like clappers
At the clattering windows, and the cold chimneys
Scatter bricks downwind, like the smoking heads
      Of dandelions.

In his threadbare barn, through
The roof like a snag-toothed graveyard the snow
Cradles and dives onto the pitched backs
Of his cow and plowhorse each thin as hanging
Laundry, and it drifts deep on their spines
So that one beast or other, almost every winter
Lets its knees stiffly down and freezes hard
To the barn floor; but his summer employers
      Always buy him others.

For there is no one else
Handy in summer, there in winter,
And he and his can dream at pleasure,
It is said, of houses burning, and do so
All through the cold, till the spooled snakes sleeping under
The stone dairy-floor stir with the turned year,
Waken, and sliding loose in their winter skins
Like air rising through thin ice, feed themselves forth
      To inherit the earth.

BURNING MOUNTAIN

No blacker than others in winter, but
The hushed snow never arrives on that slope.
An emanation of steam on damp days,
With a faint hiss, if you listen some places,
Yes, and if you pause to notice, an odor,
Even so near the chimneyed city, these
Betray what the mountain has at heart. And all night,
Here and there, popping in and out of their holes
Like ground-hogs gone nocturnal, the shy flames.

Unnatural, but no mystery.
Many are still alive to testify
Of the miner who left his lamp hanging
Lit in the shaft and took the lift, and never
Missed a thing till, half-way home to supper
The bells' clangor caught him. He was the last
You'd have expected such a thing from;
The worrying kind, whose old-womanish
Precautions had been a joke for years.

Smothered and silent, for some miles the fire
Still riddles the fissured hill, deviously
Wasting and inextinguishable. They
Have sealed off all the veins they could find,
Thus at least setting limits to it, we trust.
It consumes itself, but so slowly it will outlast
Our time and our grandchildren's, curious
But not unique: there was always one of these
Nearby, wherever we moved, when I was a child.

Under it, not far, the molten core
Of the earth recedes from its thin crust
Which all the fires we light cannot prevent
From cooling. Not a good day's walk above it
The meteors burn out in the air to fall
Harmless in empty fields, if at all.
Before long it practically seemed normal,
With its farms on it, and wells of good water,
Still cold, that should last us, and our grandchildren.

THE HOTEL-KEEPERS

All that would meet
The eyes of the hawks who slid southward
    Like paired hands, year after year,
Over the ridge bloody with autumn
    Would be the two iron roofs,
House and barn, high in the gap huddled,
    Smoke leaking from the stone stack,
A hotel sign from one hook dangling,
    And the vacant wagon-track
Trailing across the hog-backed mountain
    With no other shack in sight
For miles. So an ignorant stranger
    Might rein up there as night fell
(Though warned by his tired horse's rearing
    At nothing near the barn door)
And stopping, never be seen after;
    Thus pedlars' wares would turn up
Here and there minus their lost pedlars;
    Hounds nosing over the slope
Far downwind would give tongue suddenly
    High and frantic, closing in
On the back door; and in the valley
    Children raucous as starlings
Would start behaving at the mention
    Of the Hotel-Man.

    Who was not tall,
Who stumped slowly, brawny in gum-boots,
    And who spoke little, they said
(Quarrymen, farmers, all the local
    Know-it-alls). Who was seen once,
When a nosey passer-by followed
    Low noises he thought were moans,
Standing with raised axe in the hayloft,
    And whose threats that time, although
Not loud, pursued the rash intruder
    For months. But who, even so,
Holed up in his squat house, five decades
    Outwintered the righteous wrath
And brute schemes they nursed in the valley,
    Accidents, as they well knew,
Siding with him, and no evidence

With them. And survived to sit,
Crumpled with age, and be visited
    Blabbing in his swivel-chair
With eyes adrift and wits dismantled,
    From sagging lip letting fall
Allusions of so little judgment
    That his hotel doors at last
Were chained up and all callers fielded
    By his anxious wife.

        A pleasant soul
Herself, they agreed: her plump features
    Vacant of malice, her eyes
Hard to abhor. And once he was crated
    And to his patient grave shrugged
(Where a weedy honor over him
    Seeded itself in no time)
They were soon fetching out their soft hearts
    To compare, calling to mind
Sickness, ruffians, the mountain winter,
    Her solitude, her sore feet,
Haling her down with all but music,
    Finally, to the valley,
To stand with bared gums, to be embraced,
    To be fussed over, dressed up
In their presents, and with kind people
    Be settled in a good house,
To turn chatty, to be astonished
    At nothing, to sit for hours
At her window facing the mountain,
    Troubled by recollections
No more than its own loosening stream
    Cracking like church pews, in spring,
Or the hawks, in fall, sailing over
    To their own rewards.

THE DRUNK IN THE FURNACE

> For a good decade
> The furnace stood in the naked gully, fireless
> And vacant as any hat. Then when it was
> No more to them than a hulking black fossil
> To erode unnoticed with the rest of the junk-hill
> By the poisonous creek, and rapidly to be added
> To their ignorance,
>
> They were afterwards astonished
> To confirm, one morning, a twist of smoke like a pale
> Resurrection, staggering out of its chewed hole,
> And to remark then other tokens that someone,
> Cosily bolted behind the eye-holed iron
> Door of the drafty burner, had there established
> His bad castle.
>
> Where he gets his spirits
> It's a mystery. But the stuff keeps him musical:
> Hammer-and-anvilling with poker and bottle
> To his jugged bellowings, till the last groaning clang
> As he collapses onto the rioting
> Springs of a litter of car-seats ranged on the grates,
> To sleep like an iron pig.
>
> In their tar-paper church
> On a text about stoke-holes that are sated never
> Their Reverend lingers. They nod and hate trespassers.
> When the furnace wakes, though, all afternoon
> Their witless offspring flock like piped rats to its siren
> Crescendo, and agape on the crumbling ridge
> Stand in a row and learn.

From The Moving Target *1963*

HOME FOR THANKSGIVING

I bring myself back from the streets that open like long
Silent laughs, and the others
Spilled into in the way of rivers breaking up, littered with words,
Crossed by cats and that sort of thing,
From the knowing wires and the aimed windows,
Well this is nice, on the third floor, in back of the bill-board
Which says Now Improved and I know what they mean,
I thread my way in and I sew myself in like money.

Well this is nice with my shoes moored by the bed
And the lights around the bill-board ticking on and off like a beacon,
I have brought myself back like many another crusty
Unbarbered vessel launched with a bottle,
From the bare regions of pure hope where
For a great part of the year it scarcely sets at all,
And from the night skies regularly filled with old movies of my fingers,
Weightless as shadows, groping in the sluices,
And from the visions of veins like arteries, and
From the months of plying
Between can and can, vacant as a pint in the morning,
While my sex grew into the only tree, a joyless evergreen,
And the winds played hell with it at night, coming as they did
Over at least one thousand miles of emptiness,
Thumping as though there were nothing but doors, insisting
"Come out," and of course I would have frozen.

Sunday, a fine day, with my ears wiped and my collar buttoned
I went for a jaunt all the way out and back on
A street car and under my hat with the dent settled
In the right place I was thinking maybe—a thought
Which I have noticed many times like a bold rat—
I should have stayed making some of those good women
Happy, for a while at least, Vera with
The eau-de-cologne and the small fat dog named Joy,
Gladys with her earrings, cooking and watery arms, the one
With the limp and the fancy sheets, some of them
Are still there I suppose, oh no,

I bring myself back avoiding in silence
Like a ship in a bottle.
I bring my bottle.
Or there was thin Pearl with the invisible hair nets, the wind would not

Have been right for them, they would have had
Their times, rugs, troubles,
They would have wanted curtains, cleanings, answers, they would have
Produced families their own and our own, hen friends and
Other considerations, my fingers sifting
The dark would have turned up other
Poverties, I bring myself
Back like a mother cat transferring her only kitten,
Telling myself secrets through my moustache,
They would have wanted to drink ship, sea, and all or
To break the bottle, well this is nice,
Oh misery, misery, misery,
You fit me from head to foot like a good grade suit of longies
Which I have worn for years and never want to take off.
I did the right thing after all.

A LETTER FROM GUSSIE

If our father were alive
The stains would not be defiling
The walls, nor the splintery porch
Be supported mostly by ants,
The garden, gone to the bad,
(Though that was purely Mother's)
Would not have poked through the broken
Window like an arm,
And you would never have dared
Behave toward me in this manner,
Like no gentleman and no brother,
Not even a card at Christmas
Last Christmas, and once again
Where are my dividends?

This is my reward
For remaining with our mother
Who always took your part,
You and your investments
With what she made me give you.
Don't you think I'd have liked
To get away also?
I had the brochures ready
And some nice things that fitted.
After all it isn't as though
You'd ever married. Oh
And the plumbing if I may say so
Would not have just lain down,
And the school children
Would not keep drilling the teeth
Which I no longer have
With their voices, and each time
I go out with a mouthful of clothespins
The pits of the hoodlums would not be
Dug nearer to the back steps.
Maybe you think my patience
Endures forever, maybe
You think I will die. The goat
If you recall I mentioned
I had for a while, died.
And Mother's canary, I
Won't pretend I was sorry.

Maybe you want me to think
You've died yourself, but I have
My information. I've told
Some people of consequence,
So anything can happen.
Don't say I didn't warn you.
I've looked long enough on the bright side,
And now I'm telling you
I won't stir from Mother's chair
Until I get an answer.
Morning noon and night
Can come and go as they please,
And the man from the funeral parlor
To change the calendars,
But I won't go to bed at all
Unless they come and make me,
And they'll have to bend me flat
Before they can put me away.

LEMUEL'S BLESSING

Let Lemuel bless with the wolf, which is a
dog without a master, but the Lord hears his
cries and feeds him in the desert.
CHRISTOPHER SMART: *Jubilate Agno*

You that know the way,
Spirit,
I bless your ears which are like cypruses on a mountain
With their roots in wisdom. Let me approach.
I bless your paws and their twenty nails which tell their own prayer
And are like dice in command of their own combinations.
Let me not be lost.
I bless your eyes for which I know no comparison.
Run with me like the horizon, for without you
I am nothing but a dog lost and hungry,
Ill-natured, untrustworthy, useless.

My bones together bless you like an orchestra of flutes.
Divert the weapons of the settlements and lead their dogs a dance.
Where a dog is shameless and wears servility
In his tail like a banner,
Let me wear the opprobrium of possessed and possessors
As a thick tail properly used
To warm my worst and my best parts. My tail and my laugh bless you.
Lead me past the error at the fork of hesitation.
Deliver me

From the ruth of the lair, which clings to me in the morning,
Painful when I move, like a trap;
Even debris has its favorite positions but they are not yours;
From the ruth of kindness, with its licked hands;
I have sniffed baited fingers and followed
Toward necessities which were not my own: it would make me
An habitué of back steps, faithful custodian of fat sheep;

From the ruth of prepared comforts, with its
Habitual dishes sporting my name and its collars and leashes of vanity;

From the ruth of approval, with its nets, kennels, and taxidermists;
It would use my guts for its own rackets and instruments, to play
    its own games and music;
Teach me to recognize its platforms, which are constructed like scaffolds;

From the ruth of known paths, which would use my feet, tail,
    and ears as curios,
My head as a nest for tame ants,
My fate as a warning.

I have hidden at wrong times for wrong reasons.
I have been brought to bay. More than once.
Another time, if I need it,
Create a little wind like a cold finger between my shoulders, then
Let my nails pour out a torrent of aces like grain from a threshing machine;
Let fatigue, weather, habitation, the old bones, finally,
Be nothing to me,
Let all lights but yours be nothing to me.
Let the memory of tongues not unnerve me so that I stumble or quake.
But lead me at times beside the still waters;
There when I crouch to drink let me catch a glimpse of your image
Before it is obscured with my own.

Preserve my eyes, which are irreplaceable.
Preserve my heart, veins, bones,
Against the slow death building in them like hornets until the place
    is entirely theirs.
Preserve my tongue and I will bless you again and again.

Let my ignorance and my failings
Remain far behind me like tracks made in a wet season,
At the end of which I have vanished,
So that those who track me for their own twisted ends
May be rewarded only with ignorance and failings.
But let me leave my cry stretched out behind me like a road
On which I have followed you.
And sustain me for my time in the desert
On what is essential to me.

SEPARATION

Your absence has gone through me
Like thread through a needle.
Everything I do is stitched with its color.

NOAH'S RAVEN

Why should I have returned?
My knowledge would not fit into theirs.
I found untouched the desert of the unknown,
Big enough for my feet. It is my home.
It is always beyond them. The future
Splits the present with the echo of my voice.
Hoarse with fulfillment, I never made promises.

THINGS

Possessor
At the approach of winter we are there.
Better than friends, in your sorrows we take no pleasure,
We have none of our own and no memory but yours.
We are the anchor of your future.
Patient as a border of beggars, each hand holding out its whole treasure,

We will be all the points on your compass.
We will give you interest on yourself as you deposit yourself with us.
Be a gentleman: you acquired us when you needed us,
We do what we can to please, we have some beauty, we are helpless,
Depend on us.

SAVONAROLA

Unable to endure my world and calling the failure God, I will destroy yours.

DEAD HAND

Temptations still nest in it like basilisks.
Hang it up till the rings fall.

THE SAINT OF THE UPLANDS

Their prayers still swarm on me like lost bees.
I have no sweetness. I am dust
Twice over.
              In the high barrens
The light loved us.
Their faces were hard crusts like their farms
And the eyes empty, where vision
Might not come otherwise
Than as water.

They were born to stones; I gave them
Nothing but what was theirs.
I taught them to gather the dew of their nights
Into mirrors. I hung them
Between heavens.

I took a single twig from the tree of my ignorance
And divined the living streams under
Their very houses. I showed them
The same tree growing in their dooryards.
You have ignorance of your own, I said.
They have ignorance of their own.

Over my feet they waste their few tears.

I taught them nothing.
Everywhere
The eyes are returning under the stones. And over
My dry bones they build their churches, like wells.

SIRE

Here comes the shadow not looking where it is going,
And the whole night will fall; it is time.
Here comes the little wind which the hour
Drags with it everywhere like an empty wagon through leaves.
Here comes my ignorance shuffling after them
Asking them what they are doing.

Standing still, I can hear my footsteps
Come up behind me and go on
Ahead of me and come up behind me and
With different keys clinking in the pockets,
And still I do not move. Here comes
The white-haired thistle seed stumbling past through the branches
Like a paper lantern carried by a blind man.
I believe it is the lost wisdom of my grandfather
Whose ways were his own and who died before I could ask.

Forerunner, I would like to say, silent pilot,
Little dry death, future,
Your indirections are as strange to me
As my own. I know so little that anything
You might tell me would be a revelation.

Sir, I would like to say,
It is hard to think of the good woman
Presenting you with children, like cakes,
Granting you the eye of her needle,
Standing in doorways, flinging after you
Little endearments, like rocks, or her silence
Like a whole Sunday of bells. Instead, tell me:
Which of my many incomprehensions
Did you bequeath me, and where did they take you? Standing
In the shoes of indecision, I hear them
Come up behind me and go on ahead of me
Wearing boots, on crutches, barefoot, they could never
Get together on any door-sill or destination—
The one with the assortment of smiles, the one
Jailed in himself like a forest, the one who comes
Back at evening drunk with despair and turns
Into the wrong night as though he owned it—oh small
Deaf disappearance in the dusk, in which of their shoes
Will I find myself tomorrow?

FINALLY

My dread, my ignorance, my
Self, it is time. Your imminence
Prowls the palms of my hands like sweat.
Do not now, if I rise to welcome you,
Make off like roads into the deep night.
The dogs are dead at last, the locks toothless,
The habits out of reach.
I will not be false to you tonight.

Come, no longer unthinkable. Let us share
Understanding like a family name. Bring
Integrity as a gift, something
Which I had lost, which you found on the way.
I will lay it beside us, the old knife,
While we reach our conclusions.

Come. As a man who hears a sound at the gate
Opens the window and puts out the light
The better to see out into the dark,
Look, I put it out.

TO MY BROTHER HANSON

B. *Jan. 28, 1926* D. *Jan. 28, 1926*

My elder,
Born into death like a message into a bottle,
The tide
Keeps coming in empty on the only shore.
Maybe it has lovers but it has few friends.
It is never still but it keeps its counsel, and

If I address you whose curious stars
Climbed to the tops of their houses and froze,
It is in hope of no
Answer, but as so often, merely
For want of another, for
I have seen catastrophe taking root in the mirror,
And why waste my words there?

Yes, now the roads themselves are shattered
As though they had fallen from a height, and the sky
Is cracked like varnish. Hard to believe,
Our family tree
Seems to be making its mark everywhere.
I carry my head high
On a pike that shall be nameless.

Even so, we had to give up honor entirely,
But I do what I can. I am patient
With the woes of the cupboards, and God knows—
I keep the good word close to hand like a ticket.
I feed the wounded lights in their cages.
I wake up at night on the penultimate stroke, and with
My eyes still shut I remember to turn the thorn
In the breast of the bird of darkness.
I listen to the painful song
Dropping away into sleep.

Blood
Is supposed to be thicker. You were supposed to be there
When the habits closed in pushing
Their smiles in front of them, when I was filled
With something else, like a thermometer,
When the moment of departure, standing

On one leg, like a sleeping stork, by the doorway,
Put down the other foot and opened its eye.
I
Got away this time for a while. I've come
Again to the whetted edge of myself where I
Can hear the hollow waves breaking like
Bottles in the dark. What about it? Listen, I've

Had enough of this. Is there nobody
Else in the family
To take care of the tree, to nurse the mirror,
To fix up a bite for hope when the old thing
Comes to the door,
To say to the pans of the balance
Rise up and walk?

IN THE NIGHT FIELDS

I heard the sparrows shouting "Eat, eat,"
And then the day dragged its carcass in back of the hill.
Slowly the tracks darkened.

The smoke rose steadily from no fires.
The old hunger, left in the old darkness,
Turned like a hanged knife.
I would have preferred a quiet life.
The bugs of regret began their services
Using my spine as a rosary. I left the maps
For the spiders.
Let's go, I said.

        Light of the heart,
The wheat had started lighting its lanterns,
And in every house in heaven there were lights waving
Hello good-bye. But that's
Another life.
Snug on the crumbling earth
The old bottles lay dreaming of new wine.
I picked up my breast, which had gone out.
By other lights I go looking for yours

Through the standing harvest of my lost arrows.
Under the moon the shadow
Practices mowing. Not for me, I say,
Please not for my
Benefit. A man cannot live by bread
Alone.

ANOTHER YEAR COME

I have nothing new to ask of you,
Future, heaven of the poor.
I am still wearing the same things.

I am still begging the same question
By the same light,
Eating the same stone,

And the hands of the clock still knock without entering.

OCTOBER

I remember how I would say, "I will gather
These pieces together.
Any minute now I will make
A knife out of a cloud."
Even then the days
Went leaving their wounds behind them,
But, "Monument," I kept saying to the grave,
"I am still your legend."

There was another time
When our hands met and the clocks struck
And we lived on the point of a needle, like angels.

I have seen the spider's triumph
In the palm of my hand. Above
My grave, that thoroughfare,
There are words now that can bring
My eyes to my feet, tamed.
Beyond the trees wearing names that are not their own
The paths are growing like smoke.

The promises have gone,
Gone, gone, and they were here just now.
There is the sky where they laid their fish.
Soon it will be evening.

DEPARTURE'S GIRL-FRIEND

Loneliness leapt in the mirrors, but all week
I kept them covered like cages. Then I thought
Of a better thing.

And though it was late night in the city
There I was on my way
To my boat, feeling good to be going, hugging
This big wreath with the words like real
Silver: *Bon Voyage.*

    The night
Was mine but everyone's, like a birthday.
Its fur touched my face in passing. I was going
Down to my boat, my boat,
To see it off, and glad at the thought.
Some leaves of the wreath were holding my hands
And the rest waved good-bye as I walked, as though
They were still alive.

And all went well till I came to the wharf, and no one.

I say no one, but I mean
There was this young man, maybe
Out of the merchant marine,
In some uniform, and I knew who he was; just the same
When he said to me where do you think you're going,
I was happy to tell him.

But he said to me, it isn't your boat,
You don't have one. I said, it's mine, I can prove it:
Look at this wreath I'm carrying to it,
Bon Voyage. He said, this the stone wharf, lady,
You don't own anything here.
      And as I
Was turning away, the injustice of it
Lit up the buildings, and there I was
In the other and hated city
Where I was born, where nothing is moored, where
The lights crawl over the stone like flies, spelling now,
Now, and the same fate chances roll
Their many eyes; and I step once more
Through a hoop of tears and walk on, holding this

Buoy of flowers in front of my beauty,
Wishing myself the good voyage.

THE POEM

Coming late, as always,
I try to remember what I almost heard.
The light avoids my eye.

How many times have I heard the locks close
And the lark take the keys
And hang them in heaven.

THE SINGER

The song dripping from the eaves,
I know that throat

With no tongue,
Ignoring sun and moon,

That glance, that creature
Returning to its heart

By whose light the streams
Find each other.

Untameable,
Incorruptible,

In its own country
It has a gate to guard.

There arrived without choice
Take up water

And lay it on your eyes saying
Hail clarity

From now on nothing
Will appear the same

And pass through
Leaving your salt behind.

AIR

Naturally it is night.
Under the overturned lute with its
One string I am going my way
Which has a strange sound.

This way the dust, that way the dust.
I listen to both sides
But I keep right on.
I remember the leaves sitting in judgment
And then winter.

I remember the rain with its bundle of roads.
The rain taking all its roads.
Nowhere.

Young as I am, old as I am,

I forget tomorrow, the blind man.
I forget the life among the buried windows.
The eyes in the curtains.
The wall
Growing through the immortelles.
I forget silence
The owner of the smile.

This must be what I wanted to be doing,
Walking at night between the two deserts,
Singing.

BREAD AND BUTTER

I keep finding this letter
To the gods of abandon,
Tearing it up: Sirs,
Having lived in your shrines
I know what I owe you—

I don't, did I ever? With both hands
I've forgotten, I keep
Having forgotten. I'll have no such shrines here.
I will not bow in the middle of the room
To the statue of nothing
With the flies turning around it.
On these four walls I am the writing.

Why would I start such a letter?
Think of today, think of tomorrow.
Today on the tip of my tongue,
Today with my eyes,
Tomorrow the vision,
Tomorrow

In the broken window
The broken boats will come in,
The life boats
Waving their severed hands,

And I will love as I ought to
Since the beginning.

THE CROSSROADS OF THE WORLD ETC.

I would never have thought I would be born here

So late in the stone so long before morning
Between the rivers learning of salt

Memory my city

Hope my city Ignorance my city
With my teeth on your chessboard black and white
What is your name

With my dead on your
Calendar with my eyes
In your paint
Opening
With my grief on your bridges with my voice
In your stones what is your name
Typed in rain while I slept

The books just give
The names of locks
The old books names of old locks
Some have stopped beating

Photos of
Dead doors left to right still hide
The beginning
Which do you
Open if
Any
My shadow crosses them trying to strike a light

Today is in another street

I'm coming to that
Before me

The bird of the end with its
Colorless feet
Has walked on windows

I lose the track but I find it
Again again
Memory

In the mirrors the star called Nothing

Cuts us off

Wait for me

Ruin
My city
Oh wreck of the future out of which
The future rises
What is your name as we fall

As the mortar
Falls between the faces
As the one-legged man watching the chess game
Falls
As the moon withers in the blueprint
And from our graves these curtains blow

These clouds on which I have written
Hope

As I
Have done
Hearing the light flowing over a knife
And autumn on the posters

Hearing a shadow beating a bell
Ice cream in ambulances, a chain full of fingers
The trains on the
Trestles faster than their lights
The new scars around the bend
Arriving

Hearing the day pass talking to itself
Again
Another life

Once a key in another country
Now ignorance
Ignorance

I keep to your streets until they vanish
There is singing beyond
The addresses can I
Let it go home alone

A playing on veins a lark in a lantern

It conducts me to a raw Sabbath

On all sides bread
Has been begged, here are monuments
At their feet this
Section
The tubes tied off the cry gone

The cry
I would never have thought
The lightning rises and sets

Rust, my brothers, stone, my brothers
Hung your spirits on the high hooks
Can't reach them now

You've swallowed night I swallow night
I will swallow night
And lie among the games of papers
And the gills of nibbling
Fires

Will I

While the sky waits in the station like a man
With no place to go

Will I

I hear my feet in a tunnel but I move
Like a tear on a doorsill
It's now in my wrist

Ahead of me under
False teeth hanging from a cloud, his
Sign that digs for his house, Tomorrow,
The oldest man
Is throwing food into empty cages

Is it to me
He turns his cobweb
I go toward him extending
My shadow taking it to him
Is it to me he says no

Is it to me
He says no no I haven't time

Keep the lost garment, where would I find the owner?

BEFORE THAT

It was never there and already it's vanishing

City unhealthy pale with pictures of
    Cemeteries sifting on its windows
    Its planets with wind in their eyes searching among
    The crosses again
    At night
    In dark clothes

    It was never there

    Papers news from the desert
    Moving on or
    Lying in cages
    Wrapping for their
    Voices

    The river flowing past its other shore
    Past the No Names the windows washed at night
    And who is my
    Name for

    In my pocket
    Slowly the photographs becoming saints
    Never there

    I put out my hand and the dark falls through it
    Following a flag

    Gutters made in my time rounded with
    The wounded in mind
    The streets roped off for the affectionate
    Will do for the
    Mutilated

    If I
    Lie down in the street and that smoke comes out of me

    Who
    Was it

    It was a night like this that the ashes were made

    Before that
    Was always the fire

MY FRIENDS

My friends without shields walk on the target

It is late the windows are breaking

My friends without shoes leave
What they love
Grief moves among them as a fire among
Its bells
My friends without clocks turn
On the dial they turn
They part

My friends with names like gloves set out
Bare handed as they have lived
And nobody knows them
It is they that lay the wreaths at the milestones it is their
Cups that are found at the wells
And are then chained up

My friends without feet sit by the wall
Nodding to the lame orchestra
Brotherhood it says on the decorations
My friend without eyes sits in the rain smiling
With a nest of salt in his hand

My friends without fathers or houses hear
Doors opening in the darkness
Whose halls announce

Behold the smoke has come home

My friends and I have in common
The present a wax bell in a wax belfry
This message telling of
Metals this
Hunger for the sake of hunger this owl in the heart
And these hands one
For asking one for applause

My friends with nothing leave it behind
In a box
My friends without keys go out from the jails it is night

They take the same road they miss
Each other they invent the same banner in the dark
They ask their way only of sentries too proud to breathe

At dawn the stars on their flag will vanish

The water will turn up their footprints and the day will rise
Like a monument to my
Friends the forgotten

THE MAN WHO WRITES ANTS

Their eggs named for his eyes I suppose
Their eggs his tears
His memory
    Into
The ground into the walls over the sills

At each cross road
He has gone

With his days he has gone ahead
  Called by what trumpet

His words on the signs
His tears at their feet
  Growing wings

I know him from tunnels by side roads
I know him

Not his faces if he has one

I know him by his writings I am
Tempted to draw him
As I see him
Sandals stride flag on his shoulder ship on it signalling
Mask on the back of his head
Blind

Called

By what trumpet

He leaves my eyes he climbs my graves
I pass the names

He is not followed I am not following him no

Today the day of the water
With ink for my remote purpose with my pockets full of black
With no one in sight
I am walking in silence I am walking in silence I am walking
In single file listening for a trumpet

THE NEXT

The funeral procession swinging empty belts
Walks on the road on the black rain
Though the one who is dead was not ready

In the casket lid the nails are still turning

Behind it come the bearers
Of tires and wet pillows and the charred ladder
And the unrollers of torn music and a picture of smoke
And last the boy trailing the long
String cut off clean
Whom a voice follows calling Why a white one
When a red one would have done just as well

Under the casket the number
Is scratched out with signs of haste

We let it go we gather with other persuaders
In the parlor of the house of The Next
And I in my wax shoes my mind goes back
To the last dead Who was it I say

Could it have been my friend the old man
With the wet dog and the shed where he
Slept on a ladder till the whole place burned
Here just now was his other
Friend the carpenter
Who was besides a crusher of shells for cement
No they say he was months ago this was no one we knew
But he was one of us

We let it go we are
Gathered with other persuaders in the parlor
The Next is upstairs he is
Ten feet tall hale and solid his bed is no deathbed
He is surrounded by friends they enjoy the secret of safety
They are flush they are candle-lit they move to laughter
Downstairs it is not yet known
Who will go instead of him this time
Like the others one after the other because they were scared

The laughter keeps time on the stairs

These words start rising out of my wax shoes I
Say we must tell him
We must go up there we must go up there and You
Are The Next we must tell him
The persuaders say he would deafen us
When we say No no one hears us

My shoes are softening but at the same time I am saying
Someone would help us and it would be us
Even the carpenter would
Help us when he went out he said
He would not be gone long
Removing a knocker from a door
And the caskets are clearly numbered not ours we
Must rise under the turning nails
I say to the persuaders downstairs in the house of The Next

And when they say Yes no one hears them

THE STUDENTS OF JUSTICE

All night I hear the hammers
Of the blind men in the next building
Repairing their broken doors

When it is silent it is
That they are gone
Before the sun lights the way for
The young thieves

All day the blind neighbors are at their lesson
Coloring a rough book
Oh a long story
And under their white hair they keep forgetting

It tells of gorges hung with high caves and
Little rotting flags
And through the passes caravans of bugs
Bearing away our blood in pieces

What can be done what can be done

They take their hammers to the lesson

The last words so they promise me
Will be thank you and they will know why

And that night they will be allowed to move

Every day
They leave me their keys which they never use

From The Lice *1967*

THE ANIMALS

All these years behind windows
With blind crosses sweeping the tables

And myself tracking over empty ground
Animals I never saw

I with no voice

Remembering names to invent for them
Will any come back will one

Saying yes

Saying look carefully yes
We will meet again

IS THAT WHAT YOU ARE

New ghost is that what you are
Standing on the stairs of water

No longer surprised

Hope and grief are still our wings
Why we cannot fly

What failure still keeps you
Among us the unfinished

The wheels go on praying

We are not hearing something different
We beat our wings
Why are you there

I did not think I had anything else to give

The wheels say it after me

There are feathers in the ice
We lay the cold across our knees

Today the sun is farther than we think

And at the windows in the knives
You are watching

THE HYDRA

No no the dead have no brothers

The Hydra calls me but I am used to it
It calls me Everybody
But I know my name and do not answer

And you the dead
You know your names as I do not
But at moments you have just finished speaking

The snow stirs in its wrappings
Every season comes from a new place

Like your voice with its resemblances

A long time ago the lightning was practising
Something I thought was easy

I was young and the dead were in other
Ages
As the grass had its own language

Now I forget where the difference falls

One thing about the living sometimes a piece of us
Can stop dying for a moment
But you the dead

Once you go into those names you go on you never
Hesitate
You go on

THE LAST ONE

Well they'd make up their minds to be everywhere because why not.
Everywhere was theirs because they thought so.
They with two leaves they whom the birds despise.
In the middle of stones they made up their minds.
They started to cut.

Well they cut everything because why not.
Everything was theirs because they thought so.
It fell into its shadows and they took both away.
Some to have some for burning.

Well cutting everything they came to the water.
They came to the end of the day there was one left standing.
They would cut it tomorrow they went away.
The night gathered in the last branches.
The shadow of the night gathered in the shadow on the water.
The night and the shadow put on the same head.
And it said Now.

Well in the morning they cut the last one.
Like the others the last one fell into its shadow.
It fell into its shadow on the water.
They took it away its shadow stayed on the water.

Well they shrugged they started trying to get the shadow away.
They cut right to the ground the shadow stayed whole.
They laid boards on it the shadow came out on top.
They shone lights on it the shadow got blacker and clearer.
They exploded the water the shadow rocked.
They built a huge fire on the roots.
Thley sent up black smoke between the shadow and the sun.
The new shadow flowed without changing the old one.
They shrugged they went away to get stones.

They came back the shadow was growing.
They started setting up stones it was growing.
They looked the other way it went on growing.
They decided they would make a stone out of it.
They took stones to the water they poured them into the shadow.
They poured them in they poured them in the stones vanished.
The shadow was not filled it went on growing.
That was one day.

The next day was just the same it went on growing.
They did all the same things it was just the same.
They decided to take its water from under it.
They took away water they took it away the water went down.
The shadow stayed where it was before.
It went on growing it grew onto the land.
They started to scrape the shadow with machines.
When it touched the machines it stayed on them.
They started to beat the shadow with sticks.
Where it touched the sticks it stayed on them.
They started to beat the shadow with hands.
Where it touched the hands it stayed on them.
That was another day.

Well the next day started about the same it went on growing.
They pushed lights into the shadow.
Where the shadow got onto them they went out.
They began to stomp on the edge it got their feet.
And when it got their feet they fell down.
It got into eyes the eyes went blind.
The ones that fell down it grew over and they vanished.
The ones that went blind and walked into it vanished.
The ones that could see and stood still
It swallowed their shadows.
Then it swallowed them too and they vanished.
Well the others ran.

The ones that were left went away to live if it would let them.
They went as far as they could.
The lucky ones with their shadows.

IT IS MARCH

It is March and black dust falls out of the books
Soon I will be gone
The tall spirit who lodged here has
Left already
On the avenues the colorless thread lies under
Old prices

When you look back there is always the past
Even when it has vanished
But when you look forward
With your dirty knuckles and the wingless
Bird on your shoulder
What can you write

The bitterness is still rising in the old mines
The fist is coming out of the egg
The thermometers out of the mouths of the corpses

At a certain height
The tails of the kites for a moment are
Covered with footsteps

Whatever I have to do has not yet begun

CAESAR

My shoes are almost dead
And as I wait at the doors of ice
I hear the cry go up for him Caesar Caesar

But when I look out the window I see only the flatlands
And the slow vanishing of the windmills
The centuries draining the deep fields

Yet this is still my country
The thug on duty says What would you change
He looks at his watch he lifts
Emptiness out of the vases
And holds it up to examine

So it is evening
With the rain starting to fall forever

One by one he calls night out of the teeth
And at last I take up
My duty

Wheeling the president past banks of flowers
Past the feet of empty stairs
Hoping he's dead

NEWS OF THE ASSASSIN

The clock strikes one one one
Through the window in a line pass
The bees whose flower is death

Why the morning smelled of honey

Already how long it is since the harvest
The dead animal fallen all the same way

On the stroke the wheels recall
That they are water
An empty window has overtaken me

After the bees comes the smell of cigars
In the lobby of darkness

APRIL

When we have gone the stone will stop singing

April April
Sinks through the sand of names

Days to come
With no stars hidden in them

You that can wait being there

You that lose nothing
Know nothing

THE GODS

If I have complained I hope I have done with it

I take no pride in circumstances but there are
Occupations
My blind neighbor has required of me
A description of darkness
And I begin I begin but

All day I keep hearing the fighting in the valley
The blows falling as rice and
With what cause
After these centuries gone and they had
Each their mourning for each of them grief
In hueless ribbons hung on walls
That fell
Their moment
Here in the future continues to find me
Till night wells up through the earth

I
Am all that became of them
Clearly all is lost

The gods are what has failed to become of us
Now it is over we do not speak
Now the moment has gone it is dark
What is man that he should be infinite
The music of a deaf planet
The one note
Continues clearly this is

The other world
These strewn rocks belong to the wind
If it could use them

THE RIVER OF BEES

In a dream I returned to the river of bees
Five orange trees by the bridge and
Beside two mills my house
Into whose courtyard a blind man followed
The goats and stood singing
Of what was older

Soon it will be fifteen years

He was old he will have fallen into his eyes

I took my eyes
A long way to the calendars
Room after room asking how shall I live

One of the ends is made of streets
One man processions carry through it
Empty bottles their
Image of hope
It was offered to me by name

Once once and once
In the same city I was born
Asking what shall I say

He will have fallen into his mouth
Men think they are better than grass

I return to his voice rising like a forkful of hay

He was old he is not real nothing is real
Nor the noise of death drawing water

We are the echo of the future

On the door it says what to do to survive
But we were not born to survive
Only to live

THE WIDOW

How easily the ripe grain
Leaves the husk
At the simple turning of the planet

There is no season
That requires us

Masters of forgetting
Threading the eyeless rocks with
A narrow light

In which ciphers wake and evil
Gets itself the face of the norm
And contrives cities

The Widow rises under our fingernails
In this sky we were born we are born

And you weep wishing you were numbers
You multiply you cannot be found
You grieve
Not that heaven does not exist but
That it exists without us

You confide
In images in things that can be
Represented which is their dimension you
Require them you say This
Is real and you do not fall down and moan

Not seeing the irony in the air
Everything that does not need you is real

The Widow does not
Hear you and your cry is numberless

This is the waking landscape
Dream after dream after dream walking away through it
Invisible invisible invisible

THE CHILD

Sometimes it is inconceivable that I should be the age I am
Almost always it is a dry point in the afternoon
I cannot remember what
I am waiting for and in my astonishment I
Can hear the blood crawling over the plains
Hurrying on to arrive before dark
I try to remember my faults to make sure
One after the other but it is never
Satisfactory the list is never complete

At times night occurs to me so that I think I have been
Struck from behind I remain perfectly
Still feigning death listening for the
Assailant perhaps at last
I even sleep a little for later I have moved
I open my eyes the lanternfish have gone home in darkness
On all sides the silence is unharmed
I remember but I feel no bruise

Then there are the stories and after a while I think something
Else must connect them besides just this me
I regard myself starting the search turning
Corners in remembered metropoli
I pass skins withering in gardens that I see now
Are not familiar
And I have lost even the thread I thought I had

If I could be consistent even in destitution
The world would be revealed
While I can I try to repeat what I believe
Creatures spirits not this posture
I do not believe in knowledge as we know it
But I forget

This silence coming at intervals out of the shell of names
It must be all one person really coming at
Different hours for the same thing
If I could learn the word for yes it could teach me questions
I would see that it was itself every time and I would
Remember to say take it up like a hand
And go with it this is at last
Yourself

The child that will lead you

A DEBT

I come on the debt again this day in November

It is raining into the yellow trees
The night kept raising white birds
The fowls of darkness entering winter
But I think of you seldom
You lost nothing you need entering death

I tell you the basket has woven itself over you
If there was grief it was in pencil on a wall
At no time had I asked you for anything

What did you take from me that I still owe you

Each time it is
A blind man opening his eyes

It is a true debt it can never be paid
How have you helped me
Is it with speech you that combed out your voice till the ends bled
Is it with hearing with waking of any kind
You in the wet veil that you chose it is not with memory
Not with sight of any kind not
Yet

It is a true debt it is mine alone
It is nameless
It rises from poverty
It goes out from me into the trees
Night falls

It follows a death like a candle
But the death is not yours

THE PLASTER

How unlike you
To have left the best of your writings here
Behind the plaster where they were never to be found
These stanzas of long lines into which the Welsh words
Had been flung like planks from a rough sea
How will I

Ever know now how much was not like you
And what else was committed to paper here
On the dark burst sofa where you would later die
Its back has left a white mark on the white wall and above that
Five and a half indistinct squares of daylight
Like pages in water
Slide across the blind plaster

Into which you slipped the creased writings as into a mail slot
In a shroud

This is now the house of the rain that falls from death
The sky is moving its things in from under the trees
In silence
As it must have started to do even then
There is still a pile of dirty toys and rags
In the corner where they found the children
Rolled in sleep

Other writings
Must be dissolving in the roof
Twitching black edges in cracks of the wet fireplaces
Stuck to shelves in the filthy pantry
Never to be found
What is like you now

Who were haunted all your life by the best of you
Hiding in your death

DECEMBER NIGHT

The cold slope is standing in darkness
But the south of the trees is dry to the touch

The heavy limbs climb into the moonlight bearing feathers
I came to watch these
White plants older at night
The oldest
Come first to the ruins

And I hear magpies kept awake by the moon
The water flows through its
Own fingers without end

Tonight once more
I find a single prayer and it is not for men

DECEMBER AMONG THE VANISHED

The old snow gets up and moves taking its
Birds with it

The beasts hide in the knitted walls
From the winter that lipless man
Hinges echo but nothing opens

A silence before this one
Has left its broken huts facing the pastures
Through their stone roofs the snow
And the darkness walk down

In one of them I sit with a dead shepherd
And watch his lambs

THE ROOM

I think all this is somewhere in myself
The cold room unlit before dawn
Containing a stillness such as attends death
And from a corner the sounds of a small bird trying
From time to time to fly a few beats in the dark
You would say it was dying it is immortal

DUSK IN WINTER

The sun sets in the cold without friends
Without reproaches after all it has done for us
It goes down believing in nothing
When it has gone I hear the stream running after it
It has brought its flute it is a long way

HOW WE ARE SPARED

At midsummer before dawn an orange light returns to the mountains
Like a great weight and the small birds cry out
And bear it up

THE DRAGONFLY

Hoeing the bean field here are the dragonfly's wings
From this spot the wheat once signalled
With lights *It is all here*
With these feet on it
My own
And the hoe in my shadow

PROVISION

All morning with dry instruments
The field repeats the sound
Of rain
From memory
And in the wall
The dead increase their invisible honey
It is August
The flocks are beginning to form
I will take with me the emptiness of my hands
What you do not have you find everywhere

THE HERDS

Climbing northward
At dusk when the horizon rose like a hand I would turn aside
Before dark I would stop by the stream falling through black ice
And once more celebrate our distance from men

As I lay among stones high in the starless night
Out of the many hoof tracks the sounds of herds
Would begin to reach me again
Above them their ancient sun skating far off

Sleeping by the glass mountain
I would watch the flocks of light grazing
And the water preparing its descent
To the first dead

THE MOURNER

On the south terraces of the glass palace
That has no bells
My hoe clacks in the bean rows
In the cool of the morning

At her hour
The mourner approaches on her way to the gate
A small old woman an aunt in the world
Without nephews or nieces
Her black straw hat shining like water
Floats back and forth climbing
Along the glass walls of the terraces
Bearing its purple wax rose

We nod as she passes slowly toward the palace
Her soft face with its tiny wattle flushed salmon
I hear her small soles receding
And remember the sound of the snow at night
Brushing the glass towers
In the time of the living

FOR THE ANNIVERSARY OF MY DEATH

Every year without knowing it I have passed the day
When the last fires will wave to me
And the silence will set out
Tireless traveller
Like the beam of a lightless star

Then I will no longer
Find myself in life as in a strange garment
Surprised at the earth
And the love of one woman
And the shamelessness of men
As today writing after three days of rain
Hearing the wren sing and the falling cease
And bowing not knowing to what

THE DRY STONE MASON

The mason is dead the gentle drunk
Master of dry walls
What he made of his years crosses the slopes without wavering
Upright but nameless
Ignorant in the new winter
Rubbed by running sheep
But the age of mortar has come to him

Bottles are waiting like fallen shrines
Under different trees in the rain
And stones drip where his hands left them
Leaning slightly inwards
His thirst is past

As he had no wife
The neighbors found where he kept his suit
A man with no family they sat with him
When he was carried through them they stood by their own dead
And they have buried him among the graves of the stones

IN THE WINTER OF MY
THIRTY-EIGHTH YEAR

It sounds unconvincing to say *When I was young*
Though I have long wondered what it would be like
To be me now
No older at all it seems from here
As far from myself as ever

Waking in fog and rain and seeing nothing
I imagine all the clocks have died in the night
Now no one is looking I could choose my age
It would be younger I suppose so I am older
It is there at hand I could take it
Except for the things I think I would do differently
They keep coming between they are what I am
They have taught me little I did not know when I was young

There is nothing wrong with my age now probably
It is how I have come to it
Like a thing I kept putting off as I did my youth

There is nothing the matter with speech
Just because it lent itself
To my uses

Of course there is nothing the matter with the stars
It is my emptiness among them
While they drift farther away in the invisible morning

THE ASIANS DYING

When the forests have been destroyed their darkness remains
The ash the great walker follows the possessors
Forever
Nothing they will come to is real
Nor for long
Over the watercourses
Like ducks in the time of the ducks
The ghosts of the villages trail in the sky
Making a new twilight

Rain falls into the open eyes of the dead
Again again with its pointless sound
When the moon finds them they are the color of everything

The nights disappear like bruises but nothing is healed
The dead go away like bruises
The blood vanishes into the poisoned farmlands
Pain the horizon
Remains
Overhead the seasons rock
They are paper bells
Calling to nothing living

The possessors move everywhere under Death their star
Like columns of smoke they advance into the shadows
Like thin flames with no light
They with no past
And fire their only future

PEASANT

All those years that you ate and changed
And grew under my picture
You saw nothing
It was only when I began to appear
That you said I must vanish

What could I do I thought things were real
Cruel and wise
And came and went in their names
I thought I would wait I was shrewder but you
Were dealing in something else

You were always embarrassed by what fed you
And made distances faster
Than you destroyed them
It bewitched my dreams
Like magazines I took out with the sheep
That helped to empty the hours
I tried to despise you for what you did not
Need to be able to do
If I could do it
Maybe I could have done without you

My contempt for you
You named ignorance and my admiration for you
Servility
When they were among the few things we had in common
Your trash and your poses were what I most appreciated
Just as you did
And the way you were free
Of me
But I fought in your wars
The way you could decide that things were not
And they died
The way you had reasons
Good enough for your time

When God was dying you bought him out
As you were in a position to do

Coming in the pale car through the mud and fresh dung
Unable to find the place though you had been there
Once at least before
Like the doctor
Without a moment to lose
I was somewhere
In the bargain

I was used to standing in the shade of the sky
A survivor
I had nothing you
Could use

I am taking my hands
Into the cleft wood assembled
In dry corners of abandoned barns
Beams being saved
For nothing broken doors pieces of carts
Other shadows have gone in there and
Wait
On hewn feet I follow the hopes of the owls
For a time I will

Drift down from the tool scars in a fine dust
Noticeably before rain in summer
And at the time of the first thaws
And at the sound of your frequent explosions
And when the roofs
Fall it will be a long while
Since anyone could still believe in me
Any more than if I were one of the
Immortals

It was you
That made the future
It was yours to take away
I see
Oh thousand gods
Only you are real
It is my shame that you did not
Make me
I am bringing up my children to be you

FOR A COMING EXTINCTION

Gray whale
Now that we are sending you to The End
That great god
Tell him
That we who follow you invented forgiveness
And forgive nothing

I write as though you could understand
And I could say it
One must always pretend something
Among the dying
When you have left the seas nodding on their stalks
Empty of you
Tell him that we were made
On another day

The bewilderment will diminish like an echo
Winding along your inner mountains
Unheard by us
And find its way out
Leaving behind it the future
Dead
And ours

When you will not see again
The whale calves trying the light
Consider what you will find in the black garden
And its court
The sea cows the Great Auks the gorillas
The irreplaceable hosts ranged countless
And fore-ordaining as stars
Our sacrifices
Join your word to theirs
Tell him
That it is we who are important

FLY

I have been cruel to a fat pigeon
Because he would not fly
All he wanted was to live like a friendly old man

He had let himself become a wreck filthy and confiding
Wild for his food beating the cat off the garbage
Ignoring his mate perpetually snotty at the beak
Smelling waddling having to be
Carried up the ladder at night content

Fly I said throwing him into the air
But he would drop and run back expecting to be fed
I said it again and again throwing him up
As he got worse
He let himself be picked up every time
Until I found him in the dovecote dead
Of the needless efforts

So that is what I am

Pondering his eye that could not
Conceive that I was a creature to run from

I who have always believed too much in words

WATCHERS

The mowers begin
And after this morning the fox
Will no longer glide close to the house in full day
When a breath stirs the wheat
Leaving his sounds waiting at a distance
Under a few trees

And lie out
Watching from the nodding light the birds on the roofs
The noon sleep

Perhaps nothing
For some time will cross the new size of the stubble fields
In the light
And watch us
But the day itself coming alone
From the woods with its hunger
Today a tall man saying nothing but taking notes
Tomorrow a colorless woman standing
With her reproach and her bony children
Before rain

LOOKING FOR MUSHROOMS AT SUNRISE

When it is not yet day
I am walking on centuries of dead chestnut leaves
In a place without grief
Though the oriole
Out of another life warns me
That I am awake

In the dark while the rain fell
The gold chanterelles pushed through a sleep that was not mine
Waking me
So that I came up the mountain to find them

Where they appear it seems I have been before
I recognize their haunts as though remembering
Another life

Where else am I walking even now
Looking for me

From The Carrier of Ladders
1970

TEACHERS

Pain is in this dark room like many speakers
of a costly set though mute
as here the needle and the turning

the night lengthens it is winter
a new year

what I live for I can seldom believe in
who I love I cannot go to
what I hope is always divided

but I say to myself you are not a child now
if the night is long remember your unimportance
sleep

then toward morning I dream of the first words
of books of voyages
sure tellings that did not start by justifying

yet at one time it seems
had taught me

WORDS FROM A TOTEM ANIMAL

Distance
is where we were
but empty of us and ahead of
me lying out in the rushes thinking
even the nights cannot come back to their hill
any time

_____

I would rather the wind came from outside
from mountains anywhere
from the stars from other
worlds even as
cold as it is this
ghost of mine passing
through me

_____

I know your silence
and the repetition
like that of a word in the ear of death
teaching
itself
itself
that is the sound of my running
the plea
plea that it makes
which you will never hear
oh god of beginnings
immortal

_____

I might have been right
not who I am
but all right
among the walls among the reasons
not even waiting
not seen
but now I am out in my feet
and they on their way
the old trees jump up again and again
strangers
there are no names for the rivers
for the days for the nights
I am who I am

oh lord cold as the thoughts of birds
and everyone can see me

———

Caught again and held again
again I am not a blessing
they bring me
names
that would fit anything
they bring them to me
they bring me hopes
all day I turn
making ropes
helping

———

My eyes are waiting for me
in the dusk
they are still closed
they have been waiting a long time
and I am feeling my way toward them

———

I am going up stream
taking to the water from time to time
my marks dry off the stones before morning
the dark surface
strokes the night
above its way
There are no stars
there is no grief
I will never arrive
I stumble when I remember how it was
with one foot
one foot still in a name

———

I can turn myself toward the other joys and their lights
but not find them
I can put my words into the mouths
of spirits
but they will not say them
I can run all night and win
and win

———

Dead leaves crushed grasses fallen limbs
the world is full of prayers
arrived at from
afterwards
a voice full of breaking
heard from afterwards
through all
the length of the night

———

I am never all of me
unto myself
and sometimes I go slowly
knowing that a sound one sound
is following me from world
to world
and that I die each time
before it reaches me

———

When I stop I am alone
at night sometimes it is almost good
as though I were almost there
sometimes then I see there is
in a bush beside me the same question
why are you
on this way
I said I will ask the stars
why are you falling and they answered
which of us

———

I dreamed I had no nails
no hair
I had lost one of the senses
not sure which
the soles peeled from my feet and
drifted away
clouds
It's all one
feet
stay mine
hold the world lightly

———

Stars even you
have been used
but not you
silence
blessing
calling me when I am lost

Maybe I will come
to where I am one
and find
I have been waiting there
as a new
year finds the song of the nuthatch

Send me out into another life
lord because this one is growing faint
I do not think it goes all the way

THE JUDGMENT OF PARIS

Long afterwards
the intelligent could deduce what had been offered
and not recognized
and they suggest that bitterness should be confined
to the fact that the gods chose for their arbiter
a mind and character so ordinary
albeit a prince

and brought up as a shepherd
a calling he must have liked
for he had returned to it

when they stood before him
the three
naked feminine deathless
and he realized that he was clothed
in nothing but mortality
the strap of his quiver of arrows crossing
between his nipples
making it seem stranger

and he knew he must choose
and on that day

the one with the gray eyes spoke first
and whatever she said he kept
thinking he remembered
but remembered it woven with confusion and fear
the two faces that he called father
the first sight of the palace
where the brothers were strangers
and the dogs watched him and refused to know him
she made everything clear she was dazzling she
offered it to him
to have for his own but what he saw
was the scorn above her eyes
and her words of which he understood few
all said to him *Take wisdom*
take power
you will forget anyway

the one with the dark eyes spoke
and everything she said
he imagined he had once wished for
but in confusion and cowardice
the crown
of his father the crowns the crowns bowing to him
his name everywhere like grass
only he and the sea
triumphant
she made everything sound possible she was
dazzling she offered it to him
to hold high but what he saw
was the cruelty around her mouth
and her words of which he understood more
all said to him *Take pride*
take glory
you will suffer anyway

the third one the color of whose eyes
later he could not remember
spoke last and slowly and
of desire and it was his
though up until then he had been
happy with his river nymph
here was his mind
filled utterly with one girl gathering
yellow flowers
and no one like her
the words
made everything seem present
almost present
present
they said to him *Take*
her
you will lose her anyway

it was only when he reached out to the voice
as though he could take the speaker
herself
that his hand filled with
something to give
but to give to only one of the three

an apple as it is told
discord itself in a single fruit its skin
already carved
To the fairest

then a mason working above the gates of Troy
in the sunlight thought he felt the stone
shiver

in the quiver on Paris's back the head
of the arrow for Achilles' heel
smiled in its sleep

and Helen stepped from the palace to gather
as she would do every day in that season
from the grove the yellow ray flowers tall
as herself

whose roots are said to dispel pain

EDOUARD

Edouard shall we leave
tomorrow
for Verdun again
shall we set out for the great days
and never be the same
never

time
is what is left
shall we start
this time in the spring
and they lead your cows out
next week to sell at the fair
and the brambles learn to scribble
over the first field

Edouard shall we have gone
when the leaves come out
but before the heat
slows the grand marches
days like those
the heights and the dying
at thy right hand
sound a long horn
and here the bright handles
will fog over
things will break and stay broken
in the keeping of women
the sheep get lost
the barns
burn unconsoled in the darkness

Edouard what would you have given
not to go
sitting last night in by the fire
again
but shall we be the same
tomorrow night shall we not have gone
leaving the faces and nightingales
As you know we will live
and what never comes back will be
you and me

THE PIPER

It is twenty years
since I first looked for words
for me now
whose wisdom or something would stay me
I chose to
trouble myself about the onset
of this
it was remote it was grievous
it is true I was still a child

I was older then
than I hope ever to be again
that summer sweating in the attic
in the foreign country
high above the piper but hearing him
once
and never moving from my book
and the narrow
house full of pregnant women
floor above floor
waiting
in that city
where the sun was the one bell

It has taken me till now
to be able to say
even this
it has taken me this long
to know what I cannot say
where it begins
like the names of the hungry
Beginning
I am here
please
be ready to teach me
I am almost ready to learn

ENVOY FROM D'AUBIGNÉ

Go book

go
now I will let you
I open the grave
live
I will die for us both

go but come again if you can
and feed me in prison

if they ask you why
you do not boast of me
tell them as they
have forgotten
truth habitually
gives birth in private

Go without ornament
without showy garment
if there is in you any
joy
may the good find it

for the others be
a glass broken in their mouths

Child
how will you
survive with nothing but your virtue
to draw around you
when they shout Die die
who have been frightened before
the many

I think of all I wrote in my time
dew
and I am standing in dry air

Here are what flowers there are
and what hope
from my years

and the fire I carried with me

Book
burn what will not abide your light

When I consider the old ambitions
to be on many lips
meaning little there
it would be enough for me to know
who is writing this
and sleep knowing it

far from glory and its gibbets

and dream of those who drank at the icy fountain
and told the truth

THE WELL

Under the stone sky the water
waits
with all its songs inside it
the immortal
it sang once
it will sing again
the days
walk across the stone in heaven
unseen as planets at noon
while the water
watches the same night

Echoes come in like swallows
calling to it
it answers without moving
but in echoes
not in its voice
they do not say what it is
only where

It is a city to which many travellers
came with clear minds
having left everything even
heaven
to sit in the dark praying as one silence
for the resurrection

THE BLACK PLATEAU

The cows bring in the last light
the dogs praise them
one by one they proceed through the stone arch
on the chine of the hill
and their reflections in the little
cold darkening stream
and the man with the pole
then the night comes down to its roads
full of love for them

————

I go eating nothing so you will be one and clear
but then how could you drown
in this arid country of stone and dark dew
I shake you in your heavy sleep
then the sun comes
and I see you are one of the stones

————

Like a little smoke in the vault
light for going
before the dogs wake in the cracked barn
the owl has come in from his shift
the water in the stone basin has forgotten
where I touch the ashes they are cold
everything is in order

————

Kestrel and lark shimmer over the high stone
like two brothers who avoid each other
on the cliff corner I met the wind
a brother

————

Almost everything you look on great sun
has fallen into itself here
which it had climbed out of like prayers
shadows of clouds
and the clothes of old women blow over the barrens
one apple tree still blossoms for its own sake

————

The cold of the heights is not the cold of the valleys
the light moves like a wind
the figures are far away walking slowly
in little knots herding pieces of darkness
their faces remote as the plaster above deaths
in the villages

———

The upper window of a ruin
one of the old faces
many places near here
things grow old where nothing was ever a child

———

Oh blessed goat live goat blessed rat
and neither of you lost

———

There is still warmth in the goat sheds years afterwards
in the abandoned fountain a dead branch points
upwards
eaten out from inside as it appears to me
I know a new legend
this is the saint of the place his present form
another blessing in absence
when the last stone has fallen he will rise
from the water
and the butterflies will tell him what he needs to know
that happened while he was asleep

———

The beginnings and ends of days like the butts of arches
reach for roofs that have fallen
the sun up there was never enough
high in its light
the bird moves apart from his cry

THE APPROACHES

The glittering rises in flocks
suddenly in the afternoon
and hangs
voiceless above the broken
houses
the cold in the doorways
and at the silent station
the hammers
out of hearts
laid out in rows in the grass

The water is asleep
as they say
everywhere
cold cold
and at night the sky
is in many
pieces in the dark
the stars set out
and leave their light

When I wake
I say I may never
get there but should get
closer and hear the sound
seeing figures I go toward them waving
they make off
birds
no one to guide me
afraid
to the warm ruins
Canaan
where the fighting is

THE WHEELS OF THE TRAINS

They are there just the same
unnoticed for years
on dark tracks at the foot of their mountain

behind them holes in the hill
endless death of the sky
foreheads long unlit
illegibly inscribed

the cars
have been called into the air
an air that has gone
but these wait unmoved in their rust
rows of suns
for another life

ahead of them
the tracks lead out through tall milkweed
untouched

for all my travels

LACKAWANNA

Where you begin
in me
I have never seen
but I believe it now
rising dark
but clear

later when I lived where
you went past
already you were black
moving under gases by
red windows
obedient child
I shrank from you

on girders of your bridges
I ran
told to be afraid
obedient
the arches never touched you the running
shadow never
looked
the iron
and black ice never
stopped ringing under foot

terror
a truth
lived alone in the stained buildings
in the streets a smoke
an eyelid a clock
a black winter all year
like a dust
melting and freezing in silence

you flowed from under
and through the night the dead drifted down you
all the dead
what was found later no one
could recognize

told to be afraid
I wake black to the knees
so it has happened
I have set foot in you
both feet
Jordan
too long I was ashamed
at a distance

OTHER TRAVELLERS TO THE RIVER

William Bartram how many
have appeared in their sleep
climbing like flames into
your eyes
and have stood gazing out over the sire of waters
with night behind them
in the east
The tall bank where you stood
would soon crumble
you would die before they were born
they would wake not remembering
and on the river
that same day
was bearing off its empty flower again
and overhead the sounds of the earth
danced naked
thinking no one could see them

THE TRAIL INTO KANSAS

The early wagons left no sign
no smoke betrays them
line pressed in the grass *we were here*
all night the sun bleeds in us
and the wound slows us in the daytime
will it heal
there

we few
late
we gave our names to each other to keep
wrapped in their old bells
the wrappings work loose
something eats them when we sleep and wakes us
ringing

when day comes
shadows that were once ours and came back to look
stand up for a moment ahead of us
and then vanish
we know we are
watched but there is no danger
nothing that lives waits for us
nothing is eternal

we have been guided from scattered wombs
all the way here choosing choosing
which foot to put down
we are like wells moving
over the prairie
a blindness a hollow a cold source
will any be happy to see us
in the new home

WESTERN COUNTRY

Some days after so long even the sun
is foreign
I watch the exiles
their stride
stayed by their antique faith that no one
can die in exile
when all that is true is that death is not exile

Each no doubt knows a western country
half discovered
which he thinks is there because
he thinks he left it
and its names are still written in the sun
in his age and he knows them
but he will never tread their ground

At some distances I can no longer
sleep
my countrymen are more cruel than their stars
and I know what moves the long
files stretching into the mountains
each man with his gun
his feet
one finger's breadth off the ground

THE GARDENS OF ZUÑI

The one-armed explorer
could touch only half of the country
In the virgin half
the house fires give no more heat
than the stars
it has been so these many years
and there is no bleeding

He is long dead with his five fingers
and the sum of their touching
and the memory
of the other hand
his scout

that sent back no message
from where it had reached
with no lines in its palm
while he balanced
balanced
and groped on
for the virgin land

and found where it had been

HOMELAND

The sky goes on living it goes
on living the sky
with all the barbed wire of the west
in its veins
and the sun goes down
driving a stake
through the black heart of Andrew Jackson

HUCKLEBERRY WOMAN

Foreign voice woman
of unnamed origins nothing
to do with what I was taught
at night when it was nobody's
you climbed the mountain in back of the house
the thorn bushes slept
in their words
before day you put on
the bent back like a hill
the hands at the berries

and I wake only to the crying
when the wash tub has
fallen from your head and the alley
under the window is deep
in the spilled blue of far ranges
the rolling of small
starless skies and you turning
among them key
unlocking the presence
of the unlighted river
under the mountains

and I am borne with you on its
black stream
oh loss loss the grieving
feels its way upward
through daggers of stone
to stone
we let it go it
stays we share it
echoed by a wooden
coughing of oars in the dark
whether or not they are ours
we go with the sound

LITTLE HORSE

You come from some other forest
do you
little horse
think how long I have known these
deep dead leaves
without meeting you

I belong to no one
I would have wished for you if I had known how
what a long time the place was empty
even in my sleep
and loving it as I did
I could not have told what was missing

what can I show you
I will not ask you if you will stay
or if you will come again
I will not try to hold you
I hope you will come with me to where I stand
often sleeping and waking
by the patient water
that has no father nor mother

PRESIDENTS

The president of shame has his own flag
the president of lies quotes the voice
of God
as last counted
the president of loyalty recommends
blindness to the blind
oh oh
applause like the heels of the hanged
he walks on eyes
until they break
then he rides
there is no president of grief
it is a kingdom
ancient absolute with no colors
its ruler is never seen
prayers look for him
also empty flags like skins
silence the messenger runs through the vast lands
with a black mouth
open
silence the climber falls from the cliffs
with a black mouth like
a call
there is only one subject
but he is repeated
tirelessly

THE REMOVAL

To the endless tribe

I *The Procession*

When we see
the houses again
we will know that we are asleep at last

when we see
tears on the road
and they are ourselves
we are awake
the tree has been cut
on which we were leaves
the day does not know us
the river where we cross does not taste salt

the soles of our feet are black stars
but ours is the theme
of the light

II *The Homeless*

A clock keeps striking
and the echoes move in files
their faces
have been lost
flowers of salt
tongues from lost languages
doorways closed with pieces of night

III *A Survivor*

The dust never settles
but through it tongue tongue comes walking
shuffling like breath
but the old speech
is still in its country
dead

IV *The Crossing of the Removed*

At the bottom of the river
black ribbons cross under
and the water tries to soothe them
the mud tries to soothe them
the stones turn over and over trying
to comfort them
but they will not be healed
where the rims cut
and the shadows
sawed carrying
mourners
and some that had used horses
and had the harness
dropped it in half way over
on the far side the ribbons come out
invisible

V *A Widow Is Taken*

I call leave me here
the smoke on the black path
was my children
I will not walk
from the house I warmed
but they carry me through the light
my blackening face
my red eyes
everywhere I leave
one white footprint
the trackers will follow us into the cold
the water is high
the boats have been stolen away
there are no shoes
and they pretend that I am a bride
on the way to a new house

VI   *The Reflection*

Passing a broken window
they see
into each of them the wedge of blackness
pounded
it is nothing
it splits them
loose hair
bare heels
at last they are gone
filing on in vacant rooms

THE OLD ROOM

I am in the old room across from the synagogue
a dead chief hangs in the wallpaper
he is shrinking into the patch of sunlight
with its waves and nests and in the silence that follows
his death
the parade is forming again
with the street car for its band
it is forming I hear the shuffling the whispers
the choking then the grinding starts off
slowly as ice melting
they will pass by the house

closed ranks attached to the iron trolley
dragged on their backs
the black sleeves the fingers waving like banners
I am forbidden to look
but the faces are wrapped except for the eyes
darkness wells from the bandages
spreads
its loaves and fishes while on the curbs
the police the citizens
of all ages beat the muffled street with bars

what if I call *It is not me* will it stop
what if I raise an arm
to stop it
I raise an arm the whole arm stays white
dry as a beach
little winds play over it
a sunny and pleasant place I hold it
out it leaves me it goes toward them
the man in charge is a friend of the family

he smiles when he sees it he takes its hand
he gives it its bar
it drops it
I am forbidden to look

I am in the old room across from the stone star
the moon is climbing in gauze
the street is empty
except for the dark liquid running

in the tracks of ice
trying to call
Wait
but the wires are taken up with the election
there is a poll at the corner I am not to go in
but I can look in the drugstore window
where the numbers of the dead change all night on the wall
what if I vote *It is not me* will they revive
I go in my father has voted for me
I say no I will vote in my own name
I vote and the number leaps again on the wall

I am in the old room across from the night
the long scream is about to blossom
that is rooted in flames
if I called *It is not me* would it reach
through the bells

THE NIGHT OF THE SHIRTS

Oh pile of white shirts who is coming
to breathe in your shapes to carry your numbers
to appear
what hearts
are moving toward their garments here
their days
what troubles beating between arms

you look upward through
each other saying nothing has happened
and it has gone away and is sleeping
having told the same story
and we exist from within
eyes of the gods

you lie on your backs
and the wounds are not made
the blood has not heard
the boat has not turned to stone
and the dark wires to the bulb
are full of the voice of the unborn

TALE

After many winters the moss
finds the sawdust crushed bark chips
and says old friend
old friend

AS THOUGH I WAS WAITING
FOR THAT

Some day it will rain
from a cold place
and the sticks and stones will darken their faces
the salt will wash from the worn gods
of the good
and mourners will be waiting
on the far sides of the hills

and I will remember the calling
recognized at the wrong hours
long since
and hands a long way back
that will have forgotten
and a direction will have abandoned my feet
their way
that offered
itself vainly day after day
at last gone
like a color or the cloth at elbows

I will stir when it is getting dark
and stand when it is too late
as though I was waiting for that
and start out into the weather
into emptiness
passing the backs of trees
of the rain of the mourners
the backs of names the back
of darkness

for no reason
hearing no voice
with no promise
praying to myself
be clear

ASCENT

I have climbed a long way
there are my shoes
minute larvae
the dark parents
I know they will wait there looking up
until someone leads them away

by the time they have got to the place
that will do for their age
and are in there with nothing to say
the shades drawn
nothing but wear
between them

I may have reached the first
of the bare meadows
recognized in the air
the eyes by their blankness
turned
knowing myself seen by the lost
silent
barefoot choir

THE PAW

I return to my limbs with the first
gray light
and here is the gray paw under my hand
the she-wolf Perdita
has come back
to sleep beside me
her spine pressed knuckle to knuckle
down my front
her ears lying against my ribs
on the left side where the heart beats

and she takes its sound for the pulsing
of her paws
we are coursing the black sierra once more
in the starlight
oh Perdita

we are racing over the dark auroras
you and I with no shadow
with no shadow
in the same place

so she came back
again in the black hours
running before the open sack
we have run
these hours together
again
there is blood
on the paw under my fingers
flowing
there is blood then
on the black heights again
in her tracks
our tracks
but vanishing like a shadow

and there is blood
against my ribs again
oh Perdita
she is more beautiful after every wound
as though they were stars

I know
how the haunches are hollowed
stretched out in the dark
at full speed like a constellation
I hear
her breath moving on the fields of frost
my measure
I beat faster
her blood wells through my fingers
my eyes shut to see her
again
my way

before the stars fall
and the mountains go out
and the void wakes
and it is day

but we are gone

THE THREAD

Unrolling the black thread
through the tunnel
you come to the wide wall
of shoes
the soles standing
out in the air you breathe
crowded from side to side
floor to ceiling
and no names
and no door
and the bodies
stacked before them like bottles
generation upon
generation
upon generation
with their threads
asleep in their hands
and the tunnel is full
of their bodies
from there
all the way to the end of the mountain
the beginning of time
the light of day
the bird
and you are unrolling
the Sibyll's song
that is trying to reach her
beyond your dead

THE BLESSING

There is a blessing on the wide road
the egg shell road the baked highway
there is a blessing an old woman
walking fast following him

pace of a child following him

he left today
in a fast car

until or unless
she is with him
the traffic flows through her
as though she were air
or not there

she can speak only to him
she can tell him
what only he can hear

she can save him
once

it might be enough

she is hurrying

he is making good time
his breath comes more easily
he is still troubled at moments
by the feeling
that he has forgotten something
but he thinks he is escaping a terrible
horseman

BEGINNING

Long before spring
king of the black cranes
rises one day
from the black
needle's eye
on the white plain
under the white sky

the crown turns
and the eye
drilled clear through his head
turns
it is north everywhere
come out he says

come out then
the light is not yet
divided
it is a long way
to the first
anything
come even so
we will start
bring your nights with you

THE CHAFF

Those who cannot love the heavens or the earth
beaten from the heavens and the earth
eat each other
those who cannot love each other
beaten from each other
eat themselves
those who cannot love themselves
beaten from themselves
eat a terrible bread
kneaded in the morning shrouded all day
baked in the dark
whose sweet smell brings the chaff flying like empty hands
through the turning sky night after night
calling with voices of young birds
to its wheat

SECOND PSALM: THE SIGNALS

When the ox-horn sounds in the buried hills
    of Iceland
    I am alone
    my shadow runs back into me to hide
    and there is not room for both of us
    and the dread
when the ox-horn sounds on the blue stairs
    where the echoes are my mother's name
    I am alone
    as milk spilled in a street
    white instrument
    white hand
    white music
when the ox-horn is raised like a feather in one
    of several rivers
    not all of which I have come to
    and the note starts toward the sea
    I am alone
    as the optic nerve of the blind
    though in front of me it is written
    This is the end of the past
    Be happy
when the ox-horn sounds from its tassels of blood
    I always seem to be opening
    a book an envelope the top of a well
    none of them mine
    a tray of gloves has been set down
    beside my hands
    I am alone
    as the hour of the stopped clock
when the ox-horn is struck by its brother
    and the low grieving denial
    gropes forth again with its black hands
    I am alone
    as one stone left to pray in the desert
    after god had unmade himself
    I am
    I still am
when the ox-horn sounds over the dead oxen
    the guns grow light in hands
    I the fearer
    try to destroy me the fearing

I am alone
as a bow that has lost its nerve
my death sinks into me to hide
as water into stones
before a great cold
when the ox-horn is raised in silence
someone's breath is moving over my face
like the flight of a fly
but I am in this world
without you
I am alone as the sadness surrounding
what has long ministered to our convenience
alone as the note of the horn
as the human voice
saddest of instruments
as a white grain of sand falling in a still sea
alone as the figure she unwove each night alone

alone
as I will be

SHORE

We turned hearing the same note
of the flute far inland unfaltering and
unknown to each other but already
wrapped in the silence that we would each wear
we left two the hills one the valley before
day entered the pearl and we drew
together as streams descend through their
darkness to the shore

there it was even then by that horn light
of an old skin to be seen approaching
out of the black the lifted prow which waves
touched and fled from on the engraved flood
the scar on the wooden breast climbing above
the breast and the after vessel gazing
up and back at the night the family
the resemblance invisible to us
as it bore in bore in rapidly
to the rocky plain the eggs of venerable
stones the leaden shingle washed and washed under
the shrieks of curlews and that unbreaking
note as of a planet

making in fast toward our eyes fixed
on the uncolored bow one massed and older
jutting in velvet hat and the gown dark
to the shingle beyond whom the sky
whitened out of the gnarled littoral
the other no nearer the waves still young
a fisherman bareheaded in boots
it is my feet that are bare and others
may have gathered behind us the fires
would have been lit at home but we no longer
see behind us

and we hear nothing above the haul
of tongues leaving the shore to the flute's
accompaniment silent flocks pass
on their black journeys it is making in
at a speed that ignores the steely elements
we are waiting waiting what it was carrying
in the early hours as we believed

it could no longer have borne living when the white
shadow gained on heaven and a figure
like the beam of a lantern seemed
to stand in the bark but now though the hollow
board is plainly nearer the light will set
soon where it first rose and we get by heart
the spot where the shingle will scrape in the night
if the keel touches

From Writings to an Unfinished Accompaniment *1973*

THEIR WEEK

The loneliness of Sundays grows
tall there as the light
and from it they weave
bells of different sizes
to hang in empty cupboards and in doorways
and from branches
like blossoms like fruit
and in barns
and in each room like lamps
like the light

they believe it was on a Sunday
that the animals were divided
so that the flood could happen
and on a Sunday that we were severed
from the animals
with a wound that never heals
but is still the gate where the nameless
cries out

they believe that everything
that is divided
was divided on a Sunday
and they weave the bells
whose echoes
are all the days in the week

OLD FLAG

When I want to tell of the laughing throne
and of how all the straw in the world
records the sounds of dancing
the man called Old Flag is there
in the doorway
and my words might be his dogs

when I want to speak of the sweet light
on a grassy shore
he is there
and my words have never forgotten the bitter
taste of his hands
the smell of grief in the hollow sleeves
the sadness
his shoes

and they run to him laughing
as though he had been away
they dance at his feet as though
before a throne

THE CURRENT

For a long time some of us
lie in the marshes like dark coats
forgetting that we are water

dust gathers all day on our closed lids
weeds grow up through us

but the eels keep trying to tell us
writing over and over in our mud
our heavenly names

and through us a thin cold current
never sleeps

its glassy feet move on until they find stones

then cloud fish call to it again
your heart is safe with us

bright fish flock to it again touch it
with their mouths say yes
have vanished

yes and black flukes wave to it
from the Lethe of the whales

SOMETHING I'VE NOT DONE

Something I've not done
is following me
I haven't done it again and again
so it has many footsteps
like a drumstick that's grown old and never been used

In late afternoon I hear it come close
at times it climbs out of a sea
onto my shoulders
and I shrug it off
losing one more chance

Every morning
it's drunk up part of my breath for the day
and knows which way
I'm going
and already it's not done there

But once more I say I'll lay hands on it
tomorrow
and add its footsteps to my heart
and its story to my regrets
and its silence to my compass

TOOL

If it's invented it will be used

maybe not for some time

then all at once
a hammer rises from under a lid
and shakes off its cold family

its one truth is stirring in its head
order order saying

and a surprised nail leaps
into darkness
that a moment before had been nothing

waiting
for the law

BREAD

Each face in the street is a slice of bread
wandering on
searching

somewhere in the light the true hunger
appears to be passing them by
they clutch

have they forgotten the pale caves
they dreamed of hiding in
their own caves
full of the waiting of their footprints
hung with the hollow marks of their groping
full of their sleep and their hiding

have they forgotten the ragged tunnels
they dreamed of following in out of the light
to hear step after step
the heart of bread
to be sustained by its dark breath
and emerge

to find themselves alone
before a wheat field
raising its radiance to the moon

HABITS

Even in the middle of the night
they go on handing me around
but it's dark and they drop more of me
and for longer

then they hang onto my memory
thinking it's theirs

even when I'm asleep they take
one or two of my eyes for their sockets
and they look around believing
that the place is home

when I wake and can feel the black lungs
flying deeper into the century
carrying me
even then they borrow
most of my tongues to tell me
that they're me
and they lend me most of my ears to hear them

A DOOR

You walk on

carrying on your shoulders
a glass door
to some house that's not been found

there's no handle

you can't insure it
can't put it down

and you pray please let me not
fall please please let
me not drop
it

because you'd drown like water
in the pieces

so you walk on with your hands frozen
to your glass wings
in the wind
while down the door in time with your feet
skies are marching
like water down the inside of a bell

those skies are looking for you
they've left everything
they want you to remember them

they want to write some last phrase
on you
you

but they keep washing off
they need your ears
you can't hear them

they need your eyes
but you can't look up
now

they need your feet oh
they need your feet
to go on

they send out their dark birds for you
each one the last
like shadows of doors calling calling
sailing
the other way

so it sounds like good-bye

SURF-CASTING

It has to be the end of the day
the hour of one star
the beach has to be a naked slab

and you have to have practised a long time
with the last moments of fish
sending them to look for the middle of the sea
until your fingers
can play back whole voyages

then you send out one
of your toes for bait
hoping it's the right evening

you have ten chances

the moon rises from the surf
your hands listen
if only the great Foot is running

if only it will strike
and you can bring it to shore

in two strides it will take you
to the emperor's palace
stamp stamp the gates will open
he will present you with half of his kingdom
and his only daughter

and the next night you will come back
to fish for the Hand

THE WHARF

From dates we can never count
our graves
cast off
our black boats our deep
hulls put out
without us

again and again we run
down onto the wharf named
for us
bringing both hands both eyes
our tongues our
breath
and the harbor is empty

but our gravestones are blowing
like clouds backward
through time to find us
they sail over us through us
back to lives that waited
for us

and we never knew

BEGGARS AND KINGS

In the evening
all the hours that weren't used
are emptied out
and the beggars are waiting to gather them up
to open them
to find the sun in each one
and teach it its beggar's name
and sing to it *It is well*
through the night

but each of us
has his own kingdom of pains
and has not yet found them all
and is sailing in search of them day and night
infallible undisputed unresting
filled with a dumb use
and its time
like a finger in a world without hands

THE UNWRITTEN

Inside this pencil
crouch words that have never been written
never been spoken
never been taught

they're hiding

they're awake in there
dark in the dark
hearing us
but they won't come out
not for love not for time not for fire

even when the dark has worn away
they'll still be there
hiding in the air
multitudes in days to come may walk through them
breathe them
be none the wiser

what script can it be
that they won't unroll
in what language
would I recognize it
would I be able to follow it
to make out the real names
of everything

maybe there aren't
many
it could be that there's only one word
and it's all we need
it's here in this pencil
every pencil in the world
is like this

DIVISION

People are divided
because the finger god
named One
was lonely
so he made for himself a brother like him

named Other One

then they were both lonely

so each made for himself four others
all twins

then they were afraid
that they would lose each other
and be lonely

so they made for themselves two hands
to hold them together

but the hands drifted apart

so they made for the hands two arms

they said Between two arms
there is always a heart

and the heart will be for us all

but the heart between them
beat two ways
already for whoever

was to come

for whoever would
come after

one by one

ASH

The church in the forest
was built of wood

the faithful carved their names by the doors
same names as ours

soldiers burned it down

the next church where the first had stood
was built of wood

with charcoal floors
names were written in black by the doors
same names as ours

soldiers burned it down

we have a church where the others stood
it's made of ash
no roof no doors

nothing on earth
says it's ours

SIBYL

Your whole age sits between what you hear
and what you write

when you think you're getting younger
it's the voice coming closer
but only to you

so much of your words
is the words
once they've come out of the ground
and you've written them down
on petals
if it's spring

the same wind that tells you everything at once
unstitches your memory
you try to write faster than the thread is pulled
you write straight onto the air
if it's summer

with your empty needle

straight onto a face if there's light enough
straight onto hands
if it's autumn

UNDER BLACK LEAVES

In one window
old moon swollen with our shadow
bringing it
to birth one more time

in another window
one of the stars that does not know it is the south
the birds' way

the mouse is no longer afraid of me
the moth that was clinging to my face
a day in some city
has been taken away
very old it clung there forgetting everything
nails have been drawn out of my ears

certain stars leaving their doorways
hoped to become crickets
those soon to fall even threw
dice for the months
remembering some promise

that game was long before men
but the sounds travelled slowly
only now a few
arrive in the black trees
on the first night of autumn

A SICKNESS AT THE EQUINOX

September yellows
a few of the wild laurels
from wet ditches still the loosestrife
as when I was born
and the days before

I sit in late sunlight hoping to be healed
shadows of leaves slip along me
crossing my face my chest
toward the east

to each of them
in turn I say Take
it with you

take with you leaf shape
little shadow
darkness of one leaf
where you are going
a brother or sister
you were afraid was lost for good

a mother a father
a lover
a child
from under there

HORSES

The silence of a place where there were once horses
is a mountain

and I have seen by lightning that every mountain
once fell from the air
ringing
like the chime of an iron shoe

high on the cloudy slope
riders who long ago abandoned sadness
leaving its rotting fences and its grapes to fall
have entered the pass
and are gazing into the next valley

I do not see them cross over

I see that I will be lying
in the lightning on an alp of death
and out of my eyes horsemen will be riding

WORDS

When the pain of the world finds words
they sound like joy
and often we follow them
with our feet of earth
and learn them by heart
but when the joy of the world finds words
they are painful
and often we turn away
with our hands of water

SUMMITS

Mountains bloom in spring they shine in summer
they burn in autumn
but they belong to winter
every day we travel farther and at evening
we come to the same country
mountains are waiting but is it for us
all day the night was shining through them
and many of the birds were theirs

TO THE HAND

What the eye sees is a dream of sight
what it wakes to
is a dream of sight

and in the dream
for every real lock
there is only one real key
and it's in some other dream
now invisible

it's the key to the one real door
it opens the water and the sky both at once
it's already in the downward river
with my hand on it
my real hand

and I am saying to the hand
turn

open the river

FOLK ART

Sunday the fighting-cock
loses an eye
a red hand-print is plastered to its face
with a hole in it
and it sees what the palms see from the cross
one palm

EXERCISE

First forget what time it is
for an hour
do it regularly every day

then forget what day of the week it is
do this regularly for a week
then forget what country you are in
and practise doing it in company
for a week
then do them together
for a week
with as few breaks as possible

follow these by forgetting how to add
or to subtract
it makes no difference
you can change them around
after a week
both will help you later
to forget how to count

forget how to count
starting with your own age
starting with how to count backward
starting with even numbers
starting with Roman numerals
starting with fractions of Roman numerals
starting with the old calendar
going on to the old alphabet
going on to the alphabet
until everything is continuous again

go on to forgetting elements
starting with water
proceeding to earth
rising in fire

forget fire

A FLEA'S CARRYING WORDS

A flea is carrying a bag of diseases
and he says as he goes
these I did not make myself
we don't all have the same gifts
beginning isn't everything
I don't even know who made them
I don't know who'll use them
I don't use them myself
I just do what's in front of me
as I'm supposed to
I carry them
nobody likes me
nobody wants to change places with me
but I don't mind
I get away
bag and all
something needs me
everything needs me
I need myself
and the fire is my father

DOGS

Many times loneliness
is someone else
an absence
then when loneliness is no longer
someone else many times
it is someone else's dog
that you're keeping
then when the dog disappears
and the dog's absence
you are alone at last
and loneliness many times
is yourself
that absence
but at last it may be
that you are your own dog
hungry on the way
the one sound climbing a mountain
higher than time

THE WAR

There are statues moving into a war
as we move into a dream
we will never remember

they lived before us
but in the dream we may die

and each carrying
one wing as in life
we may go down all the steps of the heart
into swamp water
and draw our hands down after us
out of the names

and we may lose one by one our features
the stone may say good-bye to us
we may say good-bye to the stone
forever
and embark
like a left foot alone in the air
and hear at last voices like small bells
and be drawn ashore

and wake with the war going on

A HOLLOW

Here then is where the wolf of summer lay
heard flocks of sheep running by
like rats' teeth on the paths
heard them in the stubble like rain
listened to them pissing from their thin bones
learned one by one the tone of each jaw
grinding its dry stalks knew every cough
and by the cough the throat

here lay with the roots around him
like veins around a heart
and was the wolf of summer
there were leaves that listened to him with their whole lives
and never felt the wind
while he lay there like darkness in an ear
and hearing notes of wells
knew where the moon was

FOR SAYING THAT IT WON'T MATTER

Bones of today I am going to leave you
where you never wanted to be
listen shall we talk of it now
I am going to leave you there
every bone that is left to itself
has been in trouble
it was born to go through it
every skin is born knowing that
and each eye

you are voyaging now through the half light of my life
let us talk of this while the wind is kind
and the foam rustling on your bows
hear me I am going to leave you
on the empty shore
the sand will be blown away
we should talk about it
you were born for trouble
it is not for you that I am afraid
you will start singing camel songs

what can I say to you listen it is not for you
it won't matter to you
listen whatever you dream from then on
will be yours even if it was mine
unless it's me
listen you will still tell the fortunes of others
you will hang in the bell of earth at a wedding
you will fly on and on in white skins
by your own light

FINDING A TEACHER

In the woods I came on an old friend fishing
and I asked him a question
and he said Wait

fish were rising in the deep stream
but his line was not stirring
but I waited
it was a question about the sun

about my two eyes
my ears my mouth
my heart the earth with its four seasons
my feet where I was standing
where I was going

it slipped through my hands
as though it were water
into the river
it flowed under the trees
it sank under hulls far away
and was gone without me
then where I stood night fell

I no longer knew what to ask
I could tell that his line had no hook
I understood that I was to stay and eat with him

BALLADE OF SAYINGS

In spring if there are dogs they will bark
the sieves of the poor grow coarser
even in the dark we wake upward
each flower opens knowing the garden
water feels for water
the law has no face
nowhere are the martyrs more beautiful
the air is clear as though we should live forever

in summer if there are fleas there will be rejoicing
you kill the front of him I'll kill the back
every sieve knows a dance
each soldier is given a little bleached flag
ours are the only parents
the poor do not exist they are just the poor
the poor dream that their flowers are smaller
patience has the stones for a garden
the seer is buried at last in a gooseyard
the air is clear as though we should live forever

in autumn if there are trees eyes will open
one moment of freedom partakes of it all
those who will imitate will betray
the dogs are happy leading the archers
the hunter is hunted the dealer is dealt the listener is heard
the halls of government are the exhibition palaces of fear
anguish rusts
the poor believe that all is possible for others
each fruit hopes to give light
the air is clear as though we should live forever

in winter if there are feet bells will ring
snow falls in the bread of some and in the mouths of others
nobody listens to apologies
when prisoners clasp their hands a door locks
the days are polished with ashes
the cold lie in white tents hoarding sunrise
the poor we have with us always
the old vine stakes smell of the sea
the air is clear as though we should live forever

Prince it is said that night is one of the sieves
there is no end to how fine we shall be
at the names of the poor the eye of the needle echoes
the air is clear as though we should live forever

THE DREAMERS

In one of the dreams men tell how they woke
a man who can't read turned pages
until he came to one with his own story
it was air
and in the morning he began learning letters
starting with A is for apple
which seems wrong
he says the first letter seems wrong

a man with his eyes shut swam upward
through dark water and came to air
it was the horizon
he felt his way along it and it opened
and let the sun out so much for the sun
and in the morning he began groping for the horizon
like the hands of a clock
day and night

a man nothing but bones was singing
and one by one the notes opened
and rose in the air and were air
and he was each one
skin mouth ears feeling
feathers he keeps counting everything
aloud including himself
whatever he counts one is missing

I think I fell asleep on a doorstep
inside someone was coming
walking on white heads that were the best words I knew
and they woke at that step for the first time and were true
when I came to myself it was morning
I was at the foot of the air
in summer and I had this name
and my hand on a day of the world

SEPTEMBER

By dawn the little owls
that chattered in the red moon
have turned into magpies in the ash trees
resting between journeys
dew stays in the grass until noon
every day the mist wanders higher
to look over the old hill
and never come back
month of eyes your paths see for themselves
you have put your hand
in my hand
the green in the leaves has darkened
and begun to drift
the ivy flowers have opened
on the weasel's wall
their bees have come to them
the spiders watch with their bellies
and along all the shores
boats of the spirit are burning
without sound without smoke without flame
unseen in the sunlight
of a day under its own king

FLIES

On the day when the flies were made
death was a garden
already without walls
without apples
with nowhere to look back to
all that day the stars could be seen
black points
in the eyes of flies
and the only sound was the roar of the flies
until the sun went down

each day after that something else was made
and something else with no name
was a garden
which the flies never saw
what they saw was not there
with no end
no apples
ringed with black stars
that no one heard
and they flew in it happily all day
wearing mourning

THE SEARCH

When I look for you everything falls silent
a crowd seeing a ghost
it is true

yet I keep on trying to come toward you
looking for you
roads have been paved but many paths have gone
footprint by footprint
that led home to you
when roads already led nowhere

still I go on hoping
as I look for you
one heart walking in long dry grass
on a hill

around me birds vanish into the air
shadows flow into the ground

before me stones begin to go out like candles
guiding me

GIFT

I have to trust what was given to me
if I am to trust anything
it led the stars over the shadowless mountain
what does it not remember in its night and silence
what does it not hope knowing itself no child of time

what did it not begin what will it not end
I have to hold it up in my hands as my ribs hold up my heart
I have to let it open its wings and fly among the gifts of the unknown
again in the mountain I have to turn
to the morning

I must be led by what was given to me
as streams are led by it
and braiding flights of birds
the gropings of veins the learning of plants
the thankful days
breath by breath

I call to it Nameless One O Invisible
Untouchable Free
I am nameless I am divided
I am invisible I am untouchable
and empty
nomad live with me
be my eyes
my tongue and my hands
my sleep and my rising
out of chaos
come and be given

From The Compass Flower *1977*

THE HEART

In the first chamber of the heart
all the gloves are hanging but two
the hands are bare as they come through the door
the bell rope is moving without them
they move forward cupped as though
holding water
there is a bird bathing in their palms
in this chamber there is no color

In the second chamber of the heart
all the blindfolds are hanging but one
the eyes are open as they come in
they see the bell rope moving
without hands
they see the bathing bird
being carried forward
through the colored chamber

In the third chamber of the heart
all the sounds are hanging but one
the ears hear nothing as they come through the door
the bell rope is moving like a breath
without hands
a bird is being carried forward
bathing
in total silence

In the last chamber of the heart
all the words are hanging
but one
the blood is naked as it steps through the door
with its eyes open
and a bathing bird in its hands
and with its bare feet on the sill
moving as though on water
to the one stroke of the bell
someone is ringing without hands

THE DRIVE HOME

I was always afraid
of the time when I would arrive home
and be met by a special car
but this wasn't like that
they were so nice the young couple
and I was relieved not to be driving
so I could see the autumn leaves on the farms

I sat in the front to see better
they sat in the back
having a good time
and they laughed with their collars up
they said we could take turns driving
but when I looked
none of us was driving

then we all laughed
we wondered if anyone would notice
we talked of getting an inflatable
driver
to drive us for nothing through the autumn leaves

THE NEXT MOON

A month to the hour
since the last ear on earth
heard your voice

even then on the phone

I know the words about rest
and how you would say them
as though I myself had heard them
not long ago
but for a month I have heard nothing

and in the evening after the moon of deafness
I set foot in the proud waters
of iron and misfortune
it is a month to the hour
since you died
and it was only dusk
to the east in the garden

now it is a night street with another moon
seen for the first time but no longer new
and faces from the backs of mirrors

THE SNOW

You with no fear of dying
how you dreaded winter
the cataract forming on the green wheated hill
ice on sundial and steps and calendar
it is snowing
after you were unborn it was my turn
to carry you in a world before me
trying to imagine you
I am your parent at the beginning of winter
you are my child
we are one body
one blood
one red line melting the snow
unbroken line in falling snow

APPLES

Waking beside a pile of unsorted keys
in an empty room
the sun is high

what a long jagged string of broken bird song
they must have made as they gathered there
by the ears deaf with sleep
and the hands empty as waves
I remember the birds now
but where are the locks

when I touch the pile
my hand sounds like a wave on a shingle beach
I hear someone stirring
in the ruins of a glass mountain
after decades

those keys are so cold that they melt at my touch
all but the one
to the door of a cold morning
the colors of apples

A CONTEMPORARY

What if I came down now out of these
solid dark clouds that build up against the mountain
day after day with no rain in them
and lived as one blade of grass
in a garden in the south when the clouds part in winter
from the beginning I would be older than all the animals
and to the last I would be simpler
frost would design me and dew would disappear on me
sun would shine through me
I would be green with white roots
feel worms touch my feet as a bounty
have no name and no fear
turn naturally to the light
know how to spend the day and night
climbing out of myself
all my life

THE ESTUARY

By day we pace the many decks
of the stone boat
and at night we are turned out in its high windows
like stars of another side
taste our mouths we are the salt of the earth
salt is memory
in storm and cloud
we sleep in fine rigging like riding birds
taste our fingers
each with its own commandment
day or night it is harder to know than we know
but longer
we are asleep over charts at running windows
we are asleep with compasses in our hands
and at the bow of the stone boat
the wave from the ends of the earth keeps breaking

THE ROCK

Saxophone and subway
under waking and sleeping
then few hundred feet down nobody

sound of inner stone
with heart on fire

on top of it where it would dream
in the light on its head
and in its shadow
we know one another
riding deaf together
flying up in boxes
through gray gasses
and here pause
to breathe

all
our walls shake if we
listen
if we stop even
to rest a hand on them

when we can love it happens here too
where we tremble
who also are running like white grass
where sirens bleed through us
wires reach to us
we are bottles smashing in paper bags
and at the same time live standing in many windows
hearing under the breath the stone
that is ours alone

THE COUNTING HOUSES

Where do the hours of a city begin and end
among so many
the limits rising
and setting each time in each body
in a city how many hands of timepieces
must be counting the hours
clicking at a given moment
numbering insects into machines to be codified
calculating newsprint in the days of the living
all together they are not infinite
any more than the ignored patience
of rubber tires day and night
or the dumbness of wheels or the wires of passions

where is the horizon the avenue has not reached it
reaching and reaching lying palm upward
exposing the places where blood is given or let
at night the veins of the sleepers remember trees
countless sleepers the hours of trees
the uncounted hours the leaves in the dark
by day the light of the streets is the color of arms kept covered
and of much purpose
again at night the lights of the streets play on ceilings
they brush across walls
of room after unlit room hung with pictures
of the youth of the world

THE HELMSMEN

The navigator of day
plots his way by a few
daytime stars
which he never sees
except as black calculations
on white paper
worked out to the present
and even beyond
on a single plane
while on the same breathing voyage
the other navigator steers only
by what he sees
and he names for the visions of day
what he makes out in the dark void
over his head
he names for what he has never seen
what he will never see
and he never sees
the other
the earth itself is always between them
yet he leaves messages
concerning celestial bodies
as though he were telling of his own life
and in turn he finds
messages concerning
unseen motions of celestial bodies
movements of days of a life
and both navigators call out
passing the same places as the sunrise
and the sunset
waking and sleeping they call
but can't be sure whether they hear
increasingly they imagine echoes
year after year they
try to meet
thinking of each other constantly
and of the rumors of resemblances between them

NUMBERED APARTMENT

In every room rubber bands turn up loose
on dusty surfaces
witnesses

travellers in stopover countries
not knowing a word of the language
each of them
something in particular to do with me
who say laughing that I
was born here one William
on the last day of one September

to whom now it is again a January a Thursday
of an eleven year and
who has forgotten that
day and to whom that week is inaccessible
and this one is plain this
one

and though I say
here
I know it was not
for even at that time it was
ninety-nine streets to the north by the river
and now it is three wars back
and parents gone as though at once

the edifice in the antique
mode of kings of France
to which they took her to give birth
torn down as I
in my name was turning forty-four
and the building did not from that age go alone

into pieces wheeled away
but all through these years
rubber bands have continued to come to me
sometimes many together
arriving to accompany me although
the whole country has changed
means of travel accelerated
signs almost totally replaced traffic re-routed every

love altered
the stamps re-issued and
smells of streets and apples
moved on

the stone city in
the river has changed and of course
the river
and all words even those unread in
envelopes
all those shining cars vanished
after them entire roads gone like kite strings
incalculable records' print grown finer
just the names at that followed by smoke of numbers
and high buildings turned to glass in
other air oh one clear day

I am a different
foot of a same person in the same river
yet rubber bands lead to me and
from me across great distances
I do not recognize them coming nor remember them going
and still they continue to find me and pass like starlight

ST VINCENT'S

Thinking of rain clouds that rose over the city
on the first day of the year

in the same month
I consider that I have lived daily and with
eyes open and ears to hear
these years across from St Vincent's Hospital
above whose roof those clouds rose

its bricks by day a French red under
cross facing south
blown-up neo-classic facades the tall
dark openings between columns at
the dawn of history
exploded into many windows
in a mortised face

inside it the ambulances have unloaded
after sirens' howling nearer through traffic on
Seventh Avenue long
ago I learned not to hear them
even when the sirens stop

they turn to back in
few passers-by stay to look
and neither do I

at night two long blue
windows and one short one on the top floor
burn all night
many nights when most of the others are out
on what floor do they have
anything

I have seen the building drift moonlit through geraniums
late at night when trucks were few
moon just past the full
upper windows parts of the sky
as long as I looked
I watched it at Christmas and New Year
early in the morning I have seen the nurses ray out through
arterial streets

in the evening have noticed internes blocks away
on doorsteps one foot in the door

I have come upon the men in gloves taking out
the garbage at all hours
piling up mountains of
plastic bags white strata with green intermingled and
black
I have seen one pile
catch fire and studied the cloud
at the ends of the jets of the hoses
the fire engines as near as that
red beacons and
machine-throb heard by the whole body
I have noticed molded containers stacked outside
a delivery entrance on Twelfth Street
whether meals from a meal factory made up with those
mummified for long journeys by plane
or specimens for laboratory
examination sealed at the prescribed temperatures
either way closed delivery

and approached faces staring from above
crutches or tubular clamps
out for tentative walks
have paused for turtling wheel-chairs
heard visitors talking in wind on each corner
while the lights changed and
hot dogs were handed over at the curb
in the middle of afternoon
mustard ketchup onions and relish
and police smelling of ether and laundry
were going back

and I have known them all less than the papers of our days
smoke rises from the chimneys do they have an incinerator
what for
how warm do they believe they have to maintain the air
in there
several of the windows appear
to be made of tin
but it may be the light reflected

I have imagined bees coming and going
on those sills though I have never seen them

who was St Vincent

SUMMER NIGHT ON THE
STONE BARRENS

In the first hours of darkness
while the wide stones are still warm from the sun
through the hush waiting for thunder
a body falls out of a tree
rat or other soft skin
one beat of one heart on the bare stone
gets up and runs on
lightning flaps on the lifted horizon
both scattered beyond black leaves
nearby different cricket notes
climb and the owl cries
the worn moon will rise late among clouds
unseen larks rang at sunset
over yellow thistles of that day
I am under the ancient roof alone
the beams are held up by forgotten builders
of whom there were never pictures
I love voices not heard
but I love them
from some of them with every breath
I go farther away
and to some I return even through storm and sleep
the stillness is a black pearl
and I can see into it while the animals fall
one at a time at immeasurable intervals

SEPTEMBER PLOWING

For seasons the walled meadow
south of the house built of its stone
grows up in shepherd's purse and thistles
the weeds share April as a secret
finches disguised as summer earth
click the drying seeds
mice run over rags of parchment in August
the hare keeps looking up remembering
a hidden joy fills the songs of the cicadas

two days' rain wakes the green in the pastures
crows agree and hawks shriek with naked voices
on all sides the dark oak woods leap up and shine
the long stony meadow is plowed at last and lies
all day bare
I consider life after life as treasures
oh it is the autumn light

that brings everything back in one hand
the light again of beginnings
the amber appearing as amber

THE LOVE FOR OCTOBER

A child looking at ruins grows younger
but cold
and wants to wake to a new name
I have been younger in October
than in all the months of spring
walnut and may leaves the color
of shoulders at the end of summer
a month that has been to the mountain
and become light there
the long grass lies pointing uphill
even in death for a reason
that none of us knows
and the wren laughs in the early shade now
come again shining glance in your good time
naked air late morning
my love is for lightness
of touch foot feather
the day is yet one more yellow leaf
and without turning I kiss the light
by an old well on the last of the month
gathering wild rose hips
in the sun

AUTUMN EVENING

In the late day shining cobwebs trailed from my fingers
I could not see the far ends somewhere to the south
gold light hung for a long time in the wild clematis
called old man's beard along the warm wall
now smoke from my fire drifts across the red sun setting
half the bronze leaves still hold to the walnut trees
marjoram joy of the mountains flowers again
even in the light frosts of these nights
and there are mushrooms though the moon is new
and though shadows whiten on the grass before morning
and cowbells sound in the dusk from winter pastures

THE COIN

I have been to a fair alone
and across the river from the tented marketplace
and the church
were the green sagging balconies from which
during the occupation
the bodies of many
of the men of the town
hung for days in full view
of the women who had been their wives
I watched men in long
black coats selling animals
I watched money going
to a fat woman in white
who held pieces of white cheese
wrapped in white paper
out into the sunlight
I watched an old woman selling cut flowers
counting change
I looked at her teeth and lips
the dark kerchief on her head
there were carnations and
summer flowers rolled in wet newspaper
I considered the wares of a man
with a pile of whetstones
I watched three turtledoves eating in a cage
one of them white
one of them dyed pink
one pale blue
a coin in with their grain
pigeons watching from
the church windowsills
others flying overhead
some few bright clouds moving
all of it returns without a sound

REMEMBERING A BOATMAN

After sundown yellow sky beyond shadow mountains
range upon range in long twilight under few distant clouds
darkening pastures run into the bays
birds are already asleep high on unlit roan cliffs
straw light still flickers on the water
between two headlands in short summer
at last a long boat rowed by one man standing
appears slowly from behind a headland on the right
and starts across
too far away to hear the sounds of the wood
or see colors
a few times the wake turns up light
then I forget him for years

TALK OF FORTUNE

I meet her on the street
she says she is away a lot but it was
actually when she was living here
she came home to the apartment house
which I have just left
and inside by the mail boxes
she found a small old
woman who seemed to be trying
to open the inside door
and looked as though she had been
crying or it could have been laughing
and they tried to talk but
the old woman could not
speak more than a few words
and yet she was well dressed
even old velvet
and when the door was opened for her
she would not go in
for anything
but kept smiling and asking for
something or somebody in
another language
and when she could not make herself
understood she gave
my friend a leaf and went
away and the next day
my friend found a lot of money

THE FOUNTAIN

An old woman from the country
who sells tickets for sex shows
and looks at the buyers' faces
gave a party
in her kitchen
for her family and their friends
many of whom she did not even know
and she served everybody
yellow cake and meringues
made from her own eggs
as she told the company more than once
and no bag feed she said
she fed them on
oh yes you do grandma
said the small boy whose bed was in the corner
look she said and opened the back door
to show the hens in the evening light
scratching around the fountain

THE FLIGHT

At times in the day
I thought of a fire to watch
not that my hands were cold
but to have that doorway to see through
into the first thing
even our names are made of fire
and we feed on night
walking I thought of a fire
turning around I caught sight of it
in an opening in the wall
in another house and another
before and after
in house after house that was mine to see
the same fire the perpetual bird

From Opening the Hand *1983*

STRAWBERRIES

When my father died I saw   a narrow valley

it looked as though it began   across the river
from the landing where he was born   but there was no river

I was hoeing the sand   of a small vegetable plot
for my mother   in deepening twilight
and looked up in time   to see a farm wagon
dry and gray   horse already hidden
and no driver   going into the valley
carrying a casket

             and another wagon
coming out of the valley   behind a gray horse
with a boy driving   and a high load
of two kinds of berries   one of them strawberries

that night when I slept   I dreamed of things
wrong in the house   all of them signs
the water of the shower   running brackish
and an insect of a kind   I had seen him kill
climbing around   the walls of his bathroom
up in the morning   I stopped on the stairs
my mother was awake   already and asked me
if I wanted a shower   before breakfast
and for breakfast she said   we have strawberries

SUN AND RAIN

Opening the book   at a bright window
above a wide pasture   after five years
I find I am still standing   on a stone bridge
looking down with my mother   at dusk into a river
hearing the current as hers   in her lifetime

now it comes to me   that that was the day
she told me of seeing my father   alive for the last time
and he waved her back from the door   as she was leaving
took her hand   for a while and said
nothing

            at some signal
in a band of sunlight all the black cows   flow down the pasture together
to turn uphill and stand   as the dark rain touches them

APPARITIONS

Now it happens in these years   at unguarded intervals
with a frequency   never to be numbered
a motif surfacing in some scarcely known   music of my own
each time the beginning and   then broken off

that I will be looking down   not from a window
and once more catch a glimpse   of them hovering
above a whiteness like paper   and much nearer than I would have thought
lines of his knuckles   positions of his fingers
shadowy models of the backs   of my father's hands
that always appeared   to be different from my own

whether as to form texture   role or articulation
with a difference I granted them   from their origin
those stub fingers   as his family would term them
broad and unsprung   deflated somewhat and pallid
that I have seen stand forth one by one   obedient as dogs
so the scissors could cut   the flat nails straight across

they that whitened carrying   small piles of papers
and performed pretending   they knew how
posed with tools   held up neckties and waited
gripped their steering wheel   or my arm before striking
furnished him with complaints   concerning their skin and joints
evoked no music ever   had no comeliness
that I could recognize   when I yet supposed
that they were his alone   and were whole
what time they were younger   than mine are

or again the veins will appear   in their risen color
running over the hands   I knew as my mother's
that surprised me by pausing   so close to me
and I wait for the smell   of parsley and almonds
that I never imagined   otherwise than as hers

to float to me from the polished   translucent skin
and the lightness   of the tapering
well-kept and capable   poised small fingers
and from the platinum   wedding-band (with its gleam
of an outer planet)   that I have watched
finger and thumb of the other   hand slowly turn
and turn   while someone's voice was continuing

those hands that were always   on the way back to something
they that were shaken at the sink   and stripped the water
from each other like gloves   and dried swiftly on the dishtowel
flew above typewriter keys   faster than I could watch
faster than words   and without hesitation
appear again   and I am practicing the piano
that I have not touched   for as long as their age
one of them rises to wait   at the corner of the page
and I feel mistakes approach   that I have just learned not to make

but as I recognize   those hands they are gone
and that is what they are   as well as what they became
without belief I still watch them   wave to no one but me
across one last room   and from one receding car
it is six years now   since they touched anything
and whatever they can be said   to have held at all
spreads in widening rings   over the rimless surface

what I see then are these two   hands I remember
that wash my face   and tie my shoestrings
and have both sides   and a day around them
I do not know   how they came to me
they are nobody's children   who do they answer to
nobody told them to bleed   but their scars are my own
nobody but me   knows what they tell me
of flame and honey   and where you are
and the flow of water   the pencil in the air

BIRDIE

You don't think anything that I know of
but as for me when I think of you
I don't know how many of you there are
and I suppose you thought there was just the one

how many times you may have been born
as my father's other sisters would say
in your bawdy nobody is interested
in things like that in the family

somebody wrote down though that you was
born one time on April 20
1874 so that my grandmother
at that occasion was thirteen and the hardest thing
to believe in that account as I think of it
is that she was ever thirteen years old
the way we grew up to hide things from each other

so she had a little baby at that age

and that was you Birdie that was one of you
did you know
it presents a different picture of my
grandmother from the one I was brought up to

that was the you she had when she was thirteen
which goes a long way to explain
her puritanism and your gypsy earrings
and all the withered children who came after
and their scorn of your bright colors and your loud heart

and maybe even your son who was delicate
and an artist and painted heads of Jesus
on church walls where they crumbled and could not be moved
and your having a good time and dying in Arizona

except that as everybody knew
that you
was nothing but a mistake in
the writing and the real Birdie came along

when Grandma was into her twenties and she
had her firstborn a little baby girl
which explains nothing

puritanism earrings the children who came after
your son the frail artist the crumbling heads of Jesus
the having a good time and dying in Arizona
that was the you I met one morning in summer
whom nobody could explain for you was different

inviting all them so unexpected
and not heard of for so long your own mother
younger brother younger sisters new nephew
to breakfast laughing and waving your hands

with all the rings and them not listening
saying they was in a hurry to drive farther
and see the family and you going on
telling them everything there was to eat

YESTERDAY

My friend says I was not a good son
you understand
I say yes I understand

he says I did not go
to see my parents very often you know
and I say yes I know

even when I was living in the same city he says
maybe I would go there once
a month or maybe even less
I say oh yes

he says the last time I went to see my father
I say the last time I saw my father

he says the last time I saw my father
he was asking me about my life
how I was making out and he
went into the next room
to get something to give me

oh I say
feeling again the cold
of my father's hand the last time

he says and my father turned
in the doorway and saw me
look at my wristwatch and he
said you know I would like you to stay
and talk with me

oh yes I say

but if you are busy he said
I don't want you to feel that you
have to
just because I'm here

I say nothing

he says my father
said maybe
you have important work you are doing
or maybe you should be seeing
somebody I don't want to keep you

I look out the window
my friend is older than I am
he says and I told my father it was so
and I got up and left him then
you know

though there was nowhere I had to go
and nothing I had to do

SHAVING WITHOUT A MIRROR

As though there could be more   than one center
many skies cleared in the night   and there it is
the mountain this face of it   still brindled with cloud shadows
if I raised my hand   I could touch it like air
high shallow valleys   cradling the clear wind
all like a thing remembered   where haystacks waited for winter

but now it is so blue   would there be eyes in it
looking out from dark nerves   as the morning passes in our time
while the sound of a plane rises   behind me beyond trees
so that I breathe and reach up to the air   and feel water
it is myself   the listener to the music
to the clouds in the gray passes   and the clear leaves

where are the forest voices   now that the forests have gone
and those from above the treeline   oh where that fed on fog
of a simpler compound   that satisfied them
when did I ever knowingly   set hands on a cloud
who have walked in one often   following the rim in anger
Brother the world is blind   *and surely you come from it*
where children grow steadily   without knowledge of creatures

other than domesticated   though rags of woods yet emerge
as the clouds part and sweep on   passing southward in spring
fingers crossing the slopes   shadows running leaping
all night that peak watched   the beacon over the sea
and answered nothing   now it turns to the morning
and expression of knowledge   above immigrant woods

nothing is native of fire   and everything is born of it
then I wash my face   as usual
trying to remember a date   before the war
coming to a green farm at sunrise   dew smell from pastures
after that there were various   graduations
this passion for counting   has no root of its own
I stand by a line of trees   staring at a bare summit
do I think I was born here   I was never born

TIDAL LAGOON

From the edge of the bare reef   in the afternoon
children who can't swim   fling themselves forward calling
and disappear for a moment   in the long mirror
that contains the reflections   of the mountains

QUESTIONS TO TOURISTS STOPPED
BY A PINEAPPLE FIELD

Did you like your piece of pineapple   would you like a napkin
who gave you the pineapple   what do you know about them
do you eat much pineapple   where you come from
how did this piece compare   with pineapple you have eaten before
what do you remember about the last time   you ate a piece of pineapple
did you know where it came from   how much did it cost
do you remember the first time   you tasted pineapple
do you like it better fresh   or from the can
what do you remember   of the picture on the can
what did you feel   as you looked at the picture
which do you like better   the picture or the pineapple field
did you ever imagine   pineapples growing somewhere

how do you like   these pineapple fields
have you ever seen   pineapple fields before
do you know whether pineapple   is native to the islands
do you know whether the natives   ate pineapple
do you know whether the natives   grew pineapple
do you know how the land was acquired   to be turned into pineapple fields
do you know what is done to the land   to turn it into pineapple fields
do you know how many months   and how deeply they plow it
do you know what those machines do   are you impressed
do you know what is in those containers   are you interested

what do you think was here   before the pineapple fields
would you suppose that the fields   represent an improvement
do you think they smell better   than they did before
what is your opinion   of those square miles of black plastic
where do you think the plastic   goes when the crop is over
what do you think becomes of the land   when the crop is over
do you think the growers know best   do you think this is for your own good

what and where was the last   bird you noticed
do you remember   what sort of bird it was
do you know whether   there were birds here before
are there any birds   where you come from
do you think it matters   what do you think matters more
have you seen any   natives since you arrived
what were they doing   what were they wearing
what language were they speaking   were they in nightclubs
are there any natives   where you come from

261

have you taken pictures   of the pineapple fields
would you like for me   to hold the camera
so that you can all   be in the picture
would you mind   if I took your picture
standing in front   of those pineapple fields
do you expect   to come back

what made you decide   to come here
was this what   you came for
when did you first   hear of the islands
where were you then   how old were you
did you first see the islands   in black and white
what words were used   to describe the islands
what do the words mean   now that you are here
what do you do   for a living
what would you say is   the color of pineapple leaves
when you look at things in rows   how do you feel
would you like to dream   of pineapple fields

is this your first visit   how do you like the islands
what would you say   in your own words
you like best   about the islands
what do you want   when you take a trip
when did you get here   how long will you be staying
did you buy any clothes   especially for the islands
how much did you spend on them   before you came
was it easy to find clothes   for the islands
how much have you spent on clothes   since you got here
did you make your own plans   or are you part of a group
would you rather be on your own   or with a group
how many are in your group   how much was your ticket
are the side-tours part of the ticket   or are they extra
are hotel and meals and car   part of the ticket or extra
have you already paid   or will you pay later
did you pay by check   or by credit card
is this car rented   by the day or week

how does it compare   with the one you drive at home
how many miles   does it do to a gallon
how far do you   want to go on this island

where have you been   in the last three hours
what have you seen   in the last three miles
do you feel hurried   on your vacation
are you getting   your money's worth
how old are you   are you homesick are you well
what do you eat here   is it what you want
what gifts are you planning   to take back
how much do you expect   to spend on them
what have you bought   to take home with you
have you decided   where to put each thing
what will you say   about where they came from
what will you say   about the pineapple fields

do you like dancing here   what do you do when it rains
was this trip   purely for pleasure
do you drink more   or less than at home
how do you like   the place where you live now
were you born there   how long have you lived there
what does the name mean   is it a growth community
why are you living there   how long do you expect to stay
how old is your house   would you like to sell it

in your opinion   coming from your background
what do the islands offer   someone of your age
are there any changes   you would like to promote
would you like to invest here   would you like to live here
if so would it be year round   or just for part of the year
do you think there is a future   in pineapple

LATE WONDERS

In Los Angeles the cars are flowing
through the white air
and the news of bombings

at Universal Studios
you can ride through an avalanche
if you have never
ridden through an avalanche

with your ticket
you can ride on a trolley
before which the Red
Sea parts
just the way it did
for Moses

you can see Los Angeles
destroyed hourly
you can watch the avenue named for somewhere else
the one on which you know you are
crumple and vanish incandescent
with a terrible cry
all around you
rising from the houses and families
of everyone you have seen all day
driving shopping talking eating

it's only a movie
it's only a beam of light

SHERIDAN

The battle ended   the moment you got there

oh it was over it was over   in smoke
melted and the smoke still   washing the last away
of the shattered ends   the roaring fray
cannons gun carriages cavalry   fringes of infantry
seeping out of woods   blood bones breakage breaking
gone as though you   had just opened your eyes
and there was nobody   who saw what you had come to see
no face that realized   that you had arrived
no one in sight who knew   about you
how solid you were   General and how still
what were you doing   at last standing there
slightly smaller than life-size   in memory of yourself

this was certainly the place   there is no
place like this   this is the only place
it could have been   this unquestionably
is where the message came from   meant for you only
the touched intelligence rushing   to find you
tracing you gasping   drowning for lack of you
racing with shadows   of falling bodies
hunting you while the hours   ran and the first day
swung its long gates for cows   coming home to barnyards
fields were flooded with evening   seasons were resolved
forests came shouldering back   and the rounds
from the beginning   unrolled out of themselves
you were born and began to learn   what you learned
and it was going to find you   in your own time

with its torn phrases   to inform you
sir of your absence   to say it had happened
even then was happening   you were away
and they had broken upon   you they were long past
your picket lines they were at large   in your positions
outflanking outweighing   overruning you
burning beyond your campfires   in your constellations
while the cows gave milk   and the country slept
and you continued there   in the crystal distance
you considered yours   until the moment
when the words turned it   to colored paper
then to painted glass   then to plain lantern glass

through which you could see   as you set your left
foot in the stirrup   the enemy
you had first imagined   flashing on the farmland

and what had become of   you all that while
who were you in the war   in the only night
then hands let go the black horse   the black road opened
all its miles   the stars on your coat went out
you were hurtling into the dark   and only the horse could see
I know because afterward   it was read to me
already in bed   my mother in the chair beside me
cellos in the avenue   of a lighted city
night after night again   I listened to your ride
as somebody never there   had celebrated it
and you did not see the road   on which you were going
growing out of itself   like a fingernail
you never saw the air   you were flying through
you never heard the hoofbeats   under you

all the way hearkening   to what was not there
one continuous mumbled   thunder collapsing
on endless stairs from   so far coming in the dark yet so
sure how could it have failed   to carry to you
calling finally by name   and how could you
in the meantime have heard nothing   but it was still not
that night's battle beyond its hills   that you were hearing
and attending to   bright before you
as a furnace mouth that kept falling   back forward away
filling with hands and known faces   that flared up and crumbled
in flowing coals   to rise then and form once more
and come on again living   so that you saw them
even when the crash of cannons   was close in the dawn
and day was breaking   all around you

a line of fence ran toward you   looking familiar
a shuttered house in the mist   you thought in passing
you remembered from some other time   so you seemed to know
where you were   my God the fighting
was almost to there already   you could hear
rifles echoing just down the road   and what sounded
like shouting and you could   smell it in the morning
where your own were watching for you   coming to meet you

horses neighing   and at once the night
had not happened behind you   the whole ride
was nothing out of which they   were hurrying you
on the white horse   telling you everything
that you had not seen could not see   never would see
taking you to the place   where you dismounted
and turned to look   at what you had come for

there was the smoke   and someone with your head
raised an arm toward it   someone with your mouth
gave an order   and stepped into the century
and is seen no more   but is said
to have won that battle   survived that war
died and been buried   and only you are there
still seeing it disappear   in front of you
everyone knows the place   by your name now
the iron fence   dry drinking fountain
old faces from brick buildings   out for some sun
sidewalk drunks   corner acquaintances
leaves luminous above you   in the city night
subway station   hands at green news stand
traffic waiting   for the lights to change

THE FIELDS

Saturday on Seventh Street
full-waisted gray-haired women in Sunday sweaters
moving through the tan shades of their booths
bend over cakes they baked at home
they gaze down onto the sleep of stuffed cabbages
they stir with huge spoons sauerkraut and potato dumplings
cooked as those dishes were cooked on deep
misty plains among the sounds of horses
beside fields of black earth on the other side of the globe
that only the oldest think they remember
looking down from their windows into the world
where everybody is now

none of the young has yet wept at the smell
of cabbages
those leaves all face
none of the young after long journeys
weeks in vessels
and staring at strange coasts through fog in first light
has been recognized by the steam of sauerkraut
that is older than anyone living
so on the street they play the music
of what they do not remember
they sing of places they have not known
they dance in new costumes under the windows
in the smell of cabbages from fields
nobody has seen

JAMES

News comes that a friend far away
is dying now

I look up and see small flowers appearing
in spring grass outside the window
and can't remember their name

BERRYMAN

I will tell you what he told me
in the years just after the war
as we then called
the second world war

don't lose your arrogance yet he said
you can do that when you're older
lose it too soon and you many
merely replace it with vanity

just one time he suggested
changing the usual order
of the same words in a line of verse
why point out a thing twice

he suggested I pray to the Muse
get down on my knees and pray
right there in the corner and he
said he meant it literally

it was in the days before the beard
and the drink but he was deep
in tides of his own through which he sailed
chin sideways and head tilted like a tacking sloop

he was far older than the dates allowed for
much older than I was he was in his thirties
he snapped down his nose with an accent
I think he had affected in England

as for publishing he advised me
to paper my wall with rejection slips
his lips and the bones of his long fingers trembled
with the vehemence of his views about poetry

he said the great presence
that permitted everything and transmuted it
in poetry was passion
passion was genius and he praised movement and invention

I had hardly begun to read
I asked how can you ever be sure
that what you write is really
any good at all and he said you can't

you can't you can never be sure
you die without knowing
whether anything you wrote was any good
if you have to be sure don't write

EMIGRÉ

You will find it is
much as you imagined
in some respects
which no one can predict
you will be homesick
at times for something you can describe
and at times without being able to say
what you miss
just as you used to feel when you were at home

some will complain from the start
that you club together
with your own kind
but only those who have
done what you have done
conceived of it longed for it
lain awake waiting for it
and have come out with
no money no papers nothing
at your age
know what you have done
what you are talking about
and will find you a roof and employers

others will say from the start
that you avoid
those of your country
for a while
as your country becomes
a category in the new place
and nobody remembers the same things
in the same way
and you come to the problem
of what to remember after all
and of what is your real
language
where does it come from what does it
sound like
who speaks it

if you cling to the old usage
do you not cut yourself off
from the new speech
but if you rush to the new lips
do you not fade like a sound cut off
do you not dry up like a puddle
is the new tongue to be trusted

what of the relics of your childhood
should you bear in mind pieces
of dyed cotton and gnawed wood
lint of voices untranslatable stories
summer sunlight on dried paint
whose color continues to fade in the
growing brightness of the white afternoon
ferns on the shore of the transparent lake
or should you forget them
as you float between ageless languages
and call from one to the other who you are

WHAT IS MODERN

Are you modern

is the first
tree that comes
to mind modern
does it have modern leaves

who is modern after hours
at the glass door
of the drugstore
or
within sound of the airport

or passing the
animal pound
where once a week I
gas the animals
who is modern in bed

when
was modern born
who first was pleased
to feel modern
who first claimed the word
as a possession
saying I'm
modern

as someone might say
I'm a champion
or I'm
famous or even
as some would say I'm
rich

or I love the sound
of the clarinet
yes so do I
do you like classical
or modern

did modern
begin to be modern
was there a morning
when it was there for the first time
completely modern

is today modern
the modern sun rising
over the modern roof
of the modern hospital
revealing the modern water tanks and aerials
of the modern horizon

and modern humans
one after the other
solitary and without speaking
buying the morning paper
on the way to work

THE BLACK JEWEL

In the dark
there is only the sound of the cricket

south wind in the leaves
is the cricket
so is the surf on the shore
and the barking across the valley

the cricket never sleeps
the whole cricket is the pupil of one eye
it can run it can leap it can fly
in its back the moon
crosses the night

there is only one cricket
when I listen

the cricket lives in the unlit ground
in the roots
out of the wind
it has only the one sound

before I could talk
I heard the cricket
under the house
then I remembered summer

mice too and the blind lightning
are born hearing the cricket
dying they hear it
bodies of light turn listening to the cricket
the cricket is neither alive nor dead
the death of the cricket
is still the cricket
in the bare room the luck of the cricket
echoes

W. S. Merwin

W. S. Merwin was born in New York City in 1927 and grew up in Union City, New Jersey, and in Scranton, Pennsylvania. From 1949 to 1951 he worked as a tutor in France, Portugal, and Majorca. After that, for several years he made the greater part of his living by translating from French, Spanish, Latin and Portuguese. Since 1954 several fellowships have been of great assistance. In addition to poetry, he has written articles, chiefly for *The Nation,* and radio scripts for the BBC. He has lived in Spain, England, France, Mexico, and Hawaii, as well as New York City. His books of poetry are *A Mask for Janus* (1952), *The Dancing Bears* (1954), *Green with Beasts* (1956), *The Drunk in the Furnace* (1960), *The Moving Target* (1963), *The Lice* (1967), *The Carrier of Ladders* (1970) for which he was awarded the Pulitzer Prize, *Writings to an Unfinished Accompaniment* (1973), *The Compass Flower* (1977), *Opening the Hand* (1983), and *The Rain in the Trees* (1988) His translations include *The Poem of the Cid* (1959), *Spanish Ballads* (1960), *The Satires of Persius* (1961), *Lazarillo de Tormes* (1962), *The Song of Roland* (1963), *Selected Translations 1948–1968* (1968), for which he won the P.E.N. Translation Prize for 1968, *Transparence of the World,* a translation of his selection of poems by Jean Follain (1969), *Osip Mandelstam, Selected Poems* (with Clarence Brown) (1974) *Selected Translations 1968–1978* and *From the Spanish Morning* and *Four French Plays* (both 1985). He has also published three books of prose, *The Miner's Pale Children* (1970), *Houses and Travellers* (1977) and *Unframed Originals* (1982). In 1974 he was awarded The Fellowship of the Academy of American Poets. In 1987 he received the Governor's Award for Literature of the State of Hawaii.

PS
3563
E75
A6
1988

Merwin, W. S.
(William Stanley),
1927-

Selected poems.

$14.95

DATE		

WITHDRAWN

CARROLL COMMUNITY COLLEGE LMTS

0 0000 00912 7572

Library/Media Center
Carroll Community College
1601 Washington Road
Westminster, Maryland 21157

JUL 0 1 1992

© THE BAKER & TAYLOR CO.